CHA[...] HAANEL

The author of *The Master Key System*

THE NEW PSYCHOLOGY

Edited by Anthony R. Michalski

KALLISTI PUBLISHING
WILKES-BARRE, PA

Other books by Charles F. Haanel...

The Master Key System
The Master Key Workbook
Master Key Arcana
The Amazing Secrets of the Yogi
Mental Chemistry
A Book About You

Other books published by Kallisti Publishing...

Size Matters!
Getting Connected Through Exceptional Leadership
Road Map for National Security: Imperative for Change
Walk, Don't Run

WWW.KALLISTIPUBLISHING.COM

Kallisti Publishing
332 Center Street, Wilkes-Barre, PA 18702
Phone (877) 444-6188 • Fax (419) 781-1907
www.kallistipublishing.com

First Edition
10 9 8 7 6 5 4 3 2 1

Library of Congress Control Number: 2005931172
ISBN 0-9761111-3-6

DESIGNED AND PRINTED IN THE UNITED STATES OF AMERICA

CONTENTS

www.thenewpsychology.com

FOREWORD

It is with great pleasure that I can make available for you this wonderful book by Charles F. Haanel, *The New Psychology*. While it is a dense book that covers many different subjects, you will find yourself enthralled and reveling in your new understanding of things.

The New Psychology is quite different from Haanel's other works, most notably *The Master Key System*. In *The New Psychology*, Haanel expands on the ideas and theories behind mental science and offers to you many examples and proofs that bolsters the claims made.

While this work is almost one hundred years old, everything holds true to this day. I attempted to footnote things as extensively as possible. I am certain that when Haanel wrote this book, the people he mentioned were more than likely household names. James J. Hill, while almost unheard of today, was pretty much the "Bill Gates" of his time. I hope my footnotes help put things in perspective for you.

The New Psychology is a must for anyone who wants to understand the mental science. It is also a must for anyone who wants to thoroughly understand Haanel and his beliefs. Through his words, we can get a clearer picture of him—as a thinker, explorer, and perhaps even a visionary.

I know that you will enjoy this work. Charles F. Haanel has had a big impact on my life. It is my hope that he has one on yours as well.

Have fun…

Tony Michalski
Kallisti Publishing

www.kallistipublishing.com

PART ONE

The PSYCHOLOGY of SUCCESS

When any object or purpose is clearly held in thought, its precipitation, in tangible and visible form, is merely a question of time. The vision always precedes and itself determines the realization.

—Lillian Whiting

The man with the money consciousness is constantly attracting money. The man with the poverty consciousness is constantly attracting poverty. Both fulfill the exact conditions—by thought, word, and deed—that make the path for the thing of which they are conscious, come to them. "As a man thinketh in his heart, so is he."[1] Job said, "The thing I greatly feared has come upon me." In modern psychological language, it might better have been stated this way: "The thing I was greatly conscious of came upon me." Consciousness, or thought and faith, are mental wires by which the thing we are conscious of finds its way to us.

The family that expects burglars is the family that attracts burglars. The person who has no fear—or consciousness of burglars entering his home—is never molested. The highwayman never attacks the absolutely fearless man or person. There is something that forbids him. The man with a fearful consciousness invites attack. Just as the timid, fearful dog in the street is instinctively the target for all other dogs to attack.

Man is the architect of his own fortune. He can make or unmake himself. He can be weak or strong, rich or poor, according to the way he manipulates his consciousness and develops his inherent ability. The requires will power, determination, self-improvement through work, activity, and study. He must learn to clothe his mind with beautiful garments of strength and power. He must be willing to spend as much money, time, and patience to bring about this mental garment as he would in clothing his body, beautifully and efficiently. By fulfilling the law of faith and proper adjustment in the business world, nothing is impossible.

You have an inheritance of worth that is endless. While it is already given to you, it will only be possessed by you in so far as you make paths for it to come to you by the fulfillment of natural, mental, and Spiritual laws. Great objects and purposes in life are not obtained by haphazard methods. You need one talent only to be great and powerful. But this talent must not be wrapped up in a napkin and hidden away. It must be brought forth and used. It must be cultivated. If you would be great, discover your talent, then say to yourself: "This is one thing I do, forgetting all other things, I

---

1 The very famous quote by James Allen.

press toward the high calling of my place." You have a royal birthright. If this birthright is not used, it remains unknown.

There is success, fame, and glory at the top, for the reason that few arrive to possess the abundance. There is room for you there. There is wealth for you there. There is glory for you there. If, therefore, you desire to attain the heights, deny the lower things the right to hold your attention. With inherent power of will and desire, rise above their vibration.

Remember that the intention governs the attention. Have an ideal that is great and glorious. Let this ideal ever be beyond you. It may be necessary to create a new ideal frequently as you progress, because having arrived, it ceases to be an ideal. Study your ideal; commune with your ideal; visit with it; dream with it; let your heart be fixed upon it; let your ambition and energy carry you toward it. "Where your treasure is, there will your heart be also."[1]

The value you place on yourself speaks so loud and so forcefully that people instinctively feel it in every sentence you utter. "A man's gift maketh room for him and bringeth him before great men."[2] Have faith in yourself and you will find your gift and your gifts will exalt you and crown you with success.

But keep this faith to yourself.

Have you a great future mapped out for yourself?

Then see that you tell no man, if you would arrive.

Have you a great plan, or scheme, or invention, in the process of hatching?

Keep it to yourself. If you do not, it will be aborted.

These are your private property. Your faith in yourself, your future success, are strictly your private pictures, and no one should be allowed to see them, except yourself.

Keep these things in the womb of your brain and when they are ready to be born, the world will know of them.

---

1 Matthew 6:21
2 Proverbs 18:16.

Every building, great or small, was first a mental idea.

From the idea-state, it grew into a mental picture.

From the mental picture, it grew into a drafting, or drawing on a piece of paper.

From the paper, it grew into material expression and form by the erection of a steel or wooden frame, followed with the exterior walls of wood, brick, stone, or cement.

This is the method by which a building comes into visible expression. Every building had its mental form first, then the material form. Back of the mental form was the original idea.

Ideas come from the realm of the Invisible. Ideas accepted and approved become visible.

All big business, all great success first existed in big ideas, great plans, and cooperation with the Divine Mind of the Universe.

In visualizing, or building mental pictures of your business, always keep within the bounds of reasonable growth and development. A permanent success is usually of moderate growth and development. If you build your mental picture of success larger than reason warrants, you are very sure to fall down with it.

Premature success cannot be retained.

Visualize one thing until you attain that one thing. Then visualize a larger success until you have attained that. Then a still larger success, always keeping within the bounds of reason and always making allowance for the improbable or unforeseen emergency.

At the top there are large opportunities because few men are capable of sufficient self-development, persistence, and faith to climb to the top. The man who is now getting five hundred dollars a month will not get a thousand dollars until he can render a thousand dollars' worth of service per month.

You, yourself, are the architect of your fortune. When your real worth becomes so great and valuable as to make your services necessary, business men will seek you with tempting salaries.

You can then name your own price—and you will get it.

Be willing to invest money in mental tools.

Do anything that will develop worth.

In thus creating success for yourself, you are necessarily creating success for others because success depends, to some extent, on others. Others must succeed in order that you may have success.

Those who have nothing cannot purchase your service or product. Hence, you must stimulate success in others. The more you are successful in this the more complete will your success be.

You get what you give. In giving much you receive more because the thoughts of others give you mental momentum and in this momentum, you are carried along with the power of the great Oversoul, which is the source of all power.

The impossible is constantly being made possible because some one dared to believe that it was possible. The great inventions of the past were brought about by those who believed more than others could believe. Their faith stimulated action, study, thought, and effort. When faith is backed up by works, it brings forth fruit. This is the Universal Law.

There is still much to be accomplished by the men of faith. If you have faith, you are the one who will penetrate far into the realm of knowledge and bring forth from the unseen the new and astounding thing.

This is work for one who is brave enough to stand in the lions' den fearless and unafraid, while the lions of criticism roar with ridicule or threaten his life.

To accomplish much you must conserve your forces. You must consecrate these forces to the attainment of your ideal. The miner digs deep into the bowels of the earth, laboring assiduously, denying himself pleasure and luxuries, that he may obtain the precious metal, in order that he may secure the necessities of life in a larger and better measure.

There are mental gold mines, as well as material gold mines. The mental gold mines are penetrated by concentration, diligence, and interpenetrative thought; thus a man clothes himself with mental gold, which enables him through practical, ingenious, and legitimate methods to attract material wealth.

Hard thinking is mental mining and deep, penetrative thinking enables the thinker to convert gold in the mind into gold in the hand.

Mental mining like gold mining requires concentration.

To concentrate is to fix the attention on a common center. To centralize and intensify attention. To make the mind one-pointed.

One hundred percent attention is concentration.

Dynamite is concentrated and crystalized energy. Mind becomes dynamic when concentrated. Such a mind accomplishes wonders. The dynamic mind makes a success where other fail. This is true because it evolves and invents means and methods of attracting success. It has power to carry out it plans.

The path to success is upward and in the upward climb, there are many things to be transcended and overcome, which, like gravitation, tend to hold us down.

Many educated people are failures because their knowledge is superficial and intellectual, rather than practical and vital; it has therefore not contacted them with the source of power. Many uneducated people have attained success and honor because of that spirit within, which knows no defeat.

The impossible is constantly being made possible.

To attain the powers of the Master Mind, you must be free to think, to believe, and to practice.

The conscious repetition of any statement, commendatory, or otherwise calls forth in yourself the very quality expressed in the statement. Give your "self" a bad name, defame it, speak evil of it, and it will live up to the reputation you give it.

On the contrary, if you will remember that in reality your real "self" is perfect and ideal, because it is spiritual and that spirit can never be less than perfect. If you speak well of it and praise it, even though it seems to fail you, it will live up to the good reputation you give it, and you will eventually find that you have indeed found the "pearl of great price."

The ability to concentrate is the distinguishing mark of genius. It consists in the ability to hold the mind open to the source of limitless knowledge and thus secure mental accuracy, wisdom, knowledge, power, inspiration, and unfoldment, and avoid misdirected and undirected mind power, which are responsible for the many failures in life.

Too many enter upon the business of life in a haphazard way without definite aims or purposes. The first consideration in life should be to become familiar with Universal Laws, which govern the mental and physical planes of existence.

Using the simile of electricity, the Spirit may be likened unto high tension power; the mind to a transforming station.

When the trolly is off the wire, the condition of man is inert, uncertain, and timid; and if he ventures before he re-establishes this contact, his efforts meet with failure.

To know himself psychologically is to know how to make the necessary contact and thus apply the motive power to the problems of life with the greatest success and the least resistance.

The difference in men lies in their knowledge of the application of the laws governing this power. Unused power is not unlike hidden gold. It is of no value until discovered and applied.

Spiritual Power is convertible into any asset.

Properly directed, it will accomplish any purpose.

This power is the "pearl of great price." It is "a treasure hidden in the field, that a man discovered while plowing, and went and sold all that he had and purchased the field." It is the talent wrapped up in a napkin and hidden away that men must discover and uncover in order to accomplish anything of value.

This "pearl of great price" may be secured through the exercise of persistent, intelligent, and well-directed effort.

Man is an epitome of all the law, force, and manifestation of nature. The telephone, camera, flying machine, typewriter, all have their representation in the complex nature and make-up of man. It still remains true that "the greatest study of mankind is man."

Man is two-fold in his nature, namely, Spirit and Body. Take away the Spirit and there is left an inert mass of earthly matter. The Spirit of man has its definite laws of operation and manifestation. The study of these laws is called Psychology.

"Psycho" means Soul; "ology" means information, philosophy, or law. Psychology is, therefore, the science of the Soul.

A practical application of the laws governing in this science will enable you to find the solution to any problem in life and thus save yourself from many unhappy experiences.

When we say that a man puts his whole Spirit into his work, we mean that he allows his Spirit to direct the work he is doing. All work, all art—in fact, all undertakings in life—must have Soul in them to be successful. Soul and Spirit are practically synonymous terms, and the laws governing them are as definite, certain, and unerring in their result as the law of Mathematics.

Any person without the knowledge of geography and without the compass would have great difficulty in finding a foreign country or city. But with a knowledge of geography, possession of a compass, and the necessary means of travel, he could readily find such a destination.

With a knowledge of psychology, man is a knower on the path of life and every step he takes is in the right direction. Thus may he avoid the loss of both time and money, and to a very large extent control the conditions and experiences with which he is to meet in life.

The Universal Law is always the same, so far as offspring is concerned, each bringing forth after its own kind. This is truc on the spiritual as well as on the physical plane. The Spirit of you is the Universal Spirit extended into and manifesting through human form. You are a branch of the Infinite One in the same sense that a twig is a member of a tree or vine. It is of the same nature.

Man is more than man. All the possibilities of the Divine Self await unfoldment through him, just as the unblossomed rose, slumbering in the plant in midwinter, is brought forth in summer by the intelligence of the bush, through growth and effort.

The intelligence in the rosebush and all other flowering plants dreams of flowers in the silence. Blossoms are its glory, and lo, the spirit in the plant brings forth in its mature expression the fulfillment of its dreams.

So man longs for success, for power, for glory—these are evidences of his oneness with the Divine Being. These desires are the "hunger" that shall be fulfilled as soon as he comes into an understanding of the Universal Law by which he is governed.

Those who fail are walking in darkness or uncertainty. They are out of touch with the light, or guidance of the Universal Law. They are doing the will of the personal self rather than of the Divine Self.

They have not yet obtained the knowledge that makes them free.

The psychology of old ideals must pass. "Behold, I create all things new."[1] A psychology of new ideals is coming, and up to the present America has furnished the greatest example of that newer, diviner plan. America is the nation among the nations, and America with its high idealism and spirit of magnanimity, is creating a world sentiment that will bring about a world of nations, whose citizens shall know no more of war or rumors of war.

"One man shall not sow and another reap. The lion and the lamb shall feed together. There shall be no more crying nor weeping. There shall be no more death. The crooked places shall be made straight. The high places shall be made low, an the low places lifted up, and the desert shall bloom as the garden. And there shall be no night there nor anything that maketh afraid."[2]

---

1 Revelation 21:3-5

2 This more than likely came from the Book of Isaiah. It is not an exact quote, but there are parts there that are direct from the Book, such as "The crooked places shall be made straight." (Isaiah 40:4). Haanel has quoted Isaiah many times in his other works.

PART TWO

The LAW of ABUNDANCE

Thoughts Are Things

I hold it true that thoughts are things;
They're endowed with bodies and breath and wings
And that we send them forth to fill
The world with good results, or ill.
That which we call our secret thought
Speeds forth to earth's remotest spot,
Leaving its blessings or its woes
Like tracks behind it as it goes.
We build our future, thought by thought,
For good or ill, yet know it not.
Yet, so the universe was wrought.
Thought is another name for fate;
Choose, then, thy destiny and wait,
For love brings love and hate brings hate.

—Henry Van Dyke

Abundance is a natural law of the universe. The evidence of this law is conclusive; we see it on every hand. Everywhere nature is lavish, wasteful, extravagant. Nowhere is economy observed in any created thing. The millions and millions of trees and flowers and plants and animals and the vast scheme of reproduction where the process of creating and re-creating is forever going on, all indicate the lavishness with which nature has made provision for man. That there is an abundance for everyone is evident; but that many seem to have been separated from this supply is also evident; they have not yet come into realization of the universality of all substance and that mind is the active principle which starts causes in motion whereby we are related to the things we desire.

To control circumstances, a knowledge of certain scientific principles of mind-action is required. Such knowledge is a most valuable asset. It may be gained by degrees and put into practice as fast as learned. Power over circumstances is one of its fruits; health, harmony, and prosperity are assets upon its balance sheet. It costs only the labor of harvesting its great resources.

All wealth is the offspring of power; possessions are of value only as they confer power. Events are significant only as they affect power; all things represent certain forms and degrees of power.

The discovery of a reign of law by which this power could be made available for all human efforts marked an important epoch in human progress. It is the dividing line between superstition and intelligence; it eliminated the element of caprice in men's lives and substituted absolute, immutable universal law.

A knowledge of cause and effect as shown by the laws governing steam, electricity, chemical affinity, and gravitation enables man to plan courageously and to execute fearlessly. These laws are called Natural Laws, because they govern the physical world. But not all power is physical power; there is also mental power, and there is moral and spiritual power.

Thought is the vital force or energy that is being developed and that has produced such startling results in the last half century, as to bring about a world which would be absolutely inconceivable to a man existing only fifty or even twenty-five years ago. If such results have been secured by organizing these mental powerhouses in fifty years, what may not be expected in another fifty years?

Some will say, if these principles are true, why are we not demonstrating them; as the fundamental principle is obviously correct, why do we not get proper results? We do! We get results in exact accordance with our understanding of the law and our ability to make the proper application. We did not secure results from the laws governing electricity until someone formulated the law and showed us how to apply it. Mental action inaugurates a series of vibrations in the ether, which is the substance from which all things proceed, which in their turn induce a corresponding grosser vibration in the molecular substance until finally mechanical action is produced.

This puts us in an entirely new relation to our environment, opening possibilities hitherto undreamt, and this by an orderly sequence of law which is naturally involved in our new mental attitude.

It is clear, therefore, that thoughts of abundance will respond only to similar thoughts; the wealth of the individual is seen to be what he inherently is. Affluence within is found to be the secret of attraction for affluence without. The ability to produce is found to be the real source of wealth of the individual. It is for this reason that he who has his heart in his work is certain to meet with unbounded success. He will give and continually give, and the more he gives the more he will receive.

Thought is the energy by which the law of attraction is brought into operation, which eventually manifests in abundance in the lives of men.

The source of all power, as of all weakness, is from within; the secret of all success as well as all failure is likewise from within. All growth is an unfoldment from within. This is evident from all Nature: every plant, every animal, every human is a living testimony of this law and the error of the ages is in looking for strength or power from without.

A thorough understanding of this great law which permeates the Universe leads to the acquirement of that state of mind which develops and unfolds a creative thought which will produce magical changes in life. Golden opportunities will be strewn across your path, and the power and perception to properly utilize them will spring up within you. Friends will come unbidden, circumstances will adjust themselves to changed conditions, and you will have found the "pearl of greatest price."

Wisdom, strength, courage, and all harmonious conditions are the result of power, and we have seen that all power is from within; likewise every lack, limitation, or adverse circumstance is the result of weakness, and weakness is simply absence of power. It comes from nowhere; it is nothing. The remedy, then, is simply to develop power.

This is the key with which many are converting loss into gain, fear into courage, despair into joy, hope into fruition.

This may seem to be too good to be true, but remember that within a few years, by the touch of a button or the turn of a lever, science has placed almost infinite resources at the disposal of man. Is it not possible that there are other laws containing still greater possibilities?

Let us see what are the most powerful laws in Nature. In the mineral world, everything is solid and fixed. In the animal and vegetable kingdom, it is in a state of flux, forever changing, always being created and re-created. In the atmosphere we find heat, light, and energy. Each realm becomes finer and more spiritual as we pass from the visible to the invisible, from the coarse to the fine, from the low potentiality to the high potentiality. When we reach the invisible, we find energy in its purest and most volatile state.

And as the most powerful forces of Nature are the invisible forces, so we find that the most powerful forces of man are his invisible forces, his spiritual force, and the only way in which the spiritual forces can manifest is through the process of thinking. Thinking is the only activity that the spirit possesses, and thought is the only product of thinking.

Addition and subtraction are therefore spiritual transactions; reasoning is a spiritual process; ideas are spiritual conceptions; questions are spiritual searchlights; and logic, argument, and philosophy are parts of the spiritual machinery.

Every thought brings into action certain physical tissue, parts of the brain, nerve, or muscle. This produces an actual physical change in the construction of the tissue. Therefore it is only necessary to have a certain number of thoughts on a given subject in order to bring about a complete change in the physical organization of a man.

This is the process by which failure is changed to success. Thoughts of courage, power, inspiration, and harmony are substituted for thoughts of failure, despair, lack, limitation, and discord; and as these thoughts, the physical tissue is changed and the individual sees life in a new light. Old things have actually passed away. All things have become new. He is born again, this time born of the spirit. Life has a new meaning for him. He is reconstructed and is filled with joy, confidence, hope, and energy. He sees opportunities for success to which he was heretofore blind. He recognizes possibilities which before had no meaning for him. The thoughts of success with which he has been impregnated are radiated to those around him, and they in turn help him onward and upward; he attracts to him new and successful associates, and this in turn changes his environment; so that by this simple exercise of thought, a man changes not only himself, but his environment, circumstances, and conditions.

You will see—you must see—that we are at the dawn of a new day. That the possibilities are so wonderful, so fascinating, so limitless as to be almost bewildering. A century ago any man with an aeroplane or even a Gatling gun could have annihilated a whole army equipped with the implements of warfare then in use. So it is at present. Any man with a knowledge of the possibilities of modern metaphysics has an inconceivable advantage over the multitude.

Mind is creative and operates through the law of attraction. We are not to try to influence anyone to do what we think he should do. Each individual has a right to choose for himself, but aside from this we would be operating under the law of force, which is destructive in its nature and just the opposite of the law of attraction. A little reflection will convince you that all the great laws of nature operate in silence and that the underlying principle is the law of attraction. It is only destructive processes, such as earthquakes and catastrophes, that employ force. Nothing good is ever accomplished in that way.

To be successful, attention must invariably be directed to the creative plane; it must never be competitive. You do not wish to take anything away from anyone else; you want to create something for yourself, and what you want for yourself you are perfectly willing that everyone else should have.

You know that it is not necessary to take from one to give to another, but that the supply for all is abundant. Nature's storehouse of wealth is inexhaustible and if there seems to be a lack of supply anywhere it is only because the channels of distribution are as yet imperfect.

Abundance depends upon a recognition of the Law of Abundance. Mind is not only the creator, but the only creator of all there is. Certainly nothing can be created before we know that it can be created and then make the proper effort. There is no more electricity in the world today than there was fifty years ago, but until someone recognized that law by which it could be made of service, we received no benefit. Now that the law is understood, practically the whole world is illuminated by it. So with the Law of Abundance: It is only those who recognize the law and place themselves in harmony with it who share in its benefit.

A recognition of the Law of Abundance develops certain mental and moral qualities, among which are Courage, Loyalty, Tact, Sagacity, Individuality, and Constructiveness. These are all modes of thought, and as all thought is creative, they manifest in objective conditions corresponding with the mental condition. This is necessarily true because the ability of the individual to think is his ability to act upon the Universal Mind and bring it into manifestation. It is the process whereby the individual becomes a channel for the differentiation of the Universal. Every thought is a cause and every condition an effect.

This principle endows the individual with seemingly transcendental possibilities, among which is the mastery of conditions through the creation and recognition of opportunities. This creation of opportunity implies the existence or creation of the necessary qualities or talents that are thought forces and that result in a consciousness of power that future events cannot disturb. It is this organization of victory or success within the mind—this consciousness of power within—which constitutes the responsive harmonious action whereby we are related to the objects and purposes we seek. This is the law of attraction. This law, being the common property of all, can be exercised by any one having sufficient knowledge of its operation.

Courage is the power of the mind, which manifests in the love of mental conflict. It is a noble and lofty sentiment. It is equally fitted to command or obey—both require courage. It often has a tendency to conceal itself. There are men and women, too, who apparently exist only to do what is pleasing to others, but when the time comes and the latent will is revealed, we find under the velvet glove and iron hand, and no mistake about it. True courage is cool, calm, and collected, and is never fool-hardy, quarrelsome, ill-natured, or contentious.

Accumulation is the power to reserve and preserve a part of the supply that we are constantly receiving, so as to be in a position to take advantage of the larger opportunities that will come as soon as we are ready for them. Has it not been said, "To him that hath shall be given"? All successful business men have this quality well developed. James J. Hill[1], who died leaving an estate of over fifty-two million dollars, said, "If you want to know whether you are destined to be a success or failure in life, you can easily find out. The test is simple and it is infallible: Are you able to save money? If not, drop out. You will lose. You may think not, but you will lose as sure as you live. The seed of success is not in you." This is very good so far as it goes, but anyone who knows the biography of James J. Hill knows that he acquired his fifty-two million dollars

---

1 James J. Hill (1838-1916) started with nothing and formed a railroad empire. When asked by a newsman for the secret to his success, Mr. Hill responded, "Work, hard work, intelligent work, and then more work." Other than his railroad, Hill pursued a plethora of other businesses: coal and iron ore mining, shipping, banking and finance, agriculture, and milling. Later in life, he wrote *Highways of Progress*, which detailed his economic philosophy.

by following the exact methods we have given. In the first place, he started with nothing. He had to use his imagination to idealize the vast railroad that he projected across the western prairies. He then had to come into a recognition of the law of abundance in order to provide the ways and means for materializing it. Unless he had followed out this program, he would never had anything to save.

Accumulativeness acquires **momentum**: The more you accumulate, the more you desire; the more you desire, the more you accumulate; so that it is but a short time until the action and reaction acquire a momentum that cannot be stopped. It must, however, never be confounded with selfishness, miserliness, or penuriousness. They are perversions and will make any true progress impossible.

Constructiveness is the creative instinct of the mind. It will be readily seen that every successful business man must be able to plan, develop, or construct. In the business world, it is usually referred to as "initiative." It is not enough to go along in the beaten path. New ideas must be developed, new ways of doing things. It manifests in building, designing, planning, inventing, discovering, improving. It is a most valuable quality and must be constantly encouraged and developed. Every individual possesses it in some degree because he is a center of consciousness in that infinite and Eternal Energy from which all things proceed.

Water manifests on three planes: As ice, as water, and as steam. It is all the same compound. The only difference is the temperature, but no one would try to drive an engine with ice; convert it into steam and it easily takes up the load. So with your energy: If you want it to act on the creative plane, you will have to begin by melting the ice with the fire of imagination, and you will find the stronger the fire and the more ice you melt, the more powerful your thought will become and the easier it will be for you to materialize your desire.

Sagacity is the ability to perceive and cooperate with Natural Law. True Sagacity avoids trickery and deceit as it would leprosy; it is the product of that deep insight that enables one to penetrate into the heart of things and understand how to set causes into motion that will inevitably create successful conditions.

Tact is a very subtle and at the same time a very important factor in business success. It is very similar to intuition. To possess tact, one must have a fine feeling and must instinctively know what to say or what to do. In order to be tactful, one must possess *sympathy* and *understanding*, the understanding that is so rare, for all men see and hear and feel, but how desperately few "understand." Tact enables one to foresee what is about to happen and calculate the result of actions. Tact enables us to feel when we are in the presence of physical, mental, and moral cleanliness, for these are today invariably demanded as the price of success.

Loyalty is one of the strongest links that bond men of strength and character. It is one that can never be broken with impunity. The man who would lose his right hand rather than betray a friend will never lack friends. The man who will stand in silent guard—until death if need be—beside the shrine of confidence or friendship of those who allowed him to enter will find himself linked with a current of cosmic power that will attract desirable conditions only. It is inconceivable that such a person should ever meet with lack of any kind.

Individuality is the power to unfold our own latent possibilities, to be a law unto ourselves, to be interested in the race rather than the goal. Strong men care nothing for the flock of imitators who trot complacently behind them. They derive no satisfaction in the mere leading of large numbers or the plaudits of the mob. This pleases only petty natures and inferior minds. Individuality glories more in the unfolding of the power within than in the servility of the weakling.

Individuality is a real power inherent in all and the development and consequent expression of this power enables one to assume the responsibility of directing his own footsteps rather than stampeding after some self-assertive bellwether.

Inspiration is the art of imbibing, the art of self-realization, the art of adjusting the individual mind to that of the Universal Mind, the art of attaching the proper mechanism to the source of all power, the art of differentiating the formless into form, the art of becoming a channel for the flow of Infinite Wisdom, the art of visualizing perfection, the art of realizing the Omnipresence of

Omnipotence.

Truth is the imperative condition of all well-being. To be sure, to know the truth and to stand confidently on it, is a satisfaction beside which no other is comparable. Truth is the underlying verity, the condition precedent to every successful business or social relation.

Every act not in harmony with Truth, whether through ignorance or design, cuts the ground from under our feet, leads to discord, inevitable loss, and confusion; for while the humblest mind can accurately foretell the result of every correct action, the greatest and most profound and penetrating mind loses its way hopelessly and can form no conception of the result due to a departure from correct principles.

Those who establish within themselves the requisite elements of true success have established confidence, organized victory, and it only remains for them to take such steps from time to time as the newly-awakened thought force will direct, and herein rests the magical secret of all power.

Less than ten percent of our mental processes are conscious; the other ninety percent are subconscious and unconscious, so that he who would depend on his conscious thought alone for results is less than ten percent efficient. Those who are accomplishing anything worth while are those who are enabled to take advantage of this greater storehouse of mental wealth. It is in the vast domain of the subconscious mind that great truths are hidden, and it is here that thought finds its creative power—its power to correlate with its object, to bring out of the unseen the seen.

Those familiar with the laws of electricity understand the principle that electricity must always pass from a higher to a lower potentiality and can therefore make whatever application of the power they desire. Those not familiar with this law can effect nothing, and so with the law governing in the Mental World. Those who understand that *mind* penetrates all things, is omnipresent, and is responsive to every demand, can make use of the law and can control conditions, circumstances, and environment; the uninformed cannot use it because they do not know it.

The fruit of this knowledge is, as it were, a gift of the Gods. It is the "truth" that makes men free. Not only free from every lack and limitation, but free from sorrow, worry, and care. Is it not wonderful to realize that this law is no respecter of persons, that it makes no difference what your habit of thought may be, and that the way has been prepared?

With the realization that this mental power controls and directs every other power that exists, that it can be cultivated and developed, and that no limitation can be placed upon its activity, it will become apparent that it is the greatest fact in the world, the remedy for every ill, the solution for every difficulty, the gratification for every desire. In fact, that it is the Creator's magnificent provision for the emancipation of mankind.

PART THREE

The MASTER MIND

"Great men or masters stand like solitary towers in the Eternal City. And secret passages running deep beneath external nature give their thoughts intercourse with high Intelligence, which strengthens and controls them. And of which the laborers on the surface do not even dream."[1]

The Master Mind is within your body and soul, yet interpenetrating both. It is the Grand Man—the God Man—of each of us. It is the same in all human beings and is what is familiarly called the "I AM."

A Master is one who is not controlled or mastered by flesh, blood, the Devil, or others. He is not a subject, but a ruler. He knows, and he knows that he knows; because of this he is free and can be dominated by no one.

When you have reached the point where you are steadily mastering and overcoming and clothing your mind with more and more knowledge, you have your face toward the Light and are moving onward and upward.

Law becomes your servant and is no longer your master. You speak your thought or word accompanied with faith, will, and the proper mental picture, and your word accomplishes that whereunto it is sent. Or, in other words, the Creative Law hastens to fulfill your word.

High tension power represents direct contact with Spiritual Power and just as in the electrical world it must be reduced to a lower tension to be of practical, mechanical value, so this high tension power in man must be transformed and reduced in the Soul (or Subconscious Mind) to become of practical utility in the business world. We become masters by self-study, self control, and self-directed effort.

The thirst for the unrevealed and hidden knowledge should be so great that we are well nigh ready to welcome death to obtain it. The idols of conventionality, custom, and respectability must in no wise be allowed to become a stumbling block or barrier on the path. Everyone who has ascended to the mastery has had to come to the place where he dared to defy the thought, the judgment, and

1 Henry Wadsworth Longfellow from the opening paragraph of his novel *Kavanaugh: A Tale.*

the reason of the objective world.

The story is told of a student placing himself under the tutelage of a sage. The sage seemed indifferent and careless in his work of advancing the student. The student complained to the sage that he was not being taught. The sage said, "Very well, young man. Follow me." He led him over the hills, through the valleys and fields, and out into a lake into the deep waters. The sage then plunged the student beneath the water and held him there until all other desires of the young man were concentrated into the one all-important desire, namely air. Gold, wealth, honor, riches, and fame were no longer important to him. Finally, when nearly dead for want of breath, the sage lifted him up and said, "Young man, what did you want most when you were under the water?" The young man replied, "Air, air, air." Then his teacher said, "When you want Wisdom as badly as you wanted air, you will get it."

Intense desire, therefore, is the first requisite in becoming a Master Mind. Those who have made a mark in this world—those who have ascended to the heights—are those who desired intensely and incessantly. Those weak in desire never reach Mastery or the Heights until they become strong and soulfully passionate in desire.

The attraction and repulsion between chemicals is wholly a matter of intelligence and polarity, or, we might say love and hate. Just so, mind may be a magnetic pole to attract success, or it may be a magnetic pole to attract failure. Your mind becomes a money magnet in accordance with the manner in which you manipulate your consciousness. When it is a money magnet, every transaction apparently results in profit.

A man's commercial worth depends upon his internal worth and the effectiveness with which he can bring his internal worth into his external consciousness and activity. In other words, it is the inner gold that attracts the outer gold. It is the inner value that attracts the outer value. A man who has the consciousness of wealth and value, plussed with an equivalent knowledge, will always find a place.

Some one has said:

> Sublime is the dominion of the mind over body, that for a time can make flesh and nerve impregnable and strong sinews like steel, so that the weak become mighty. For a well-regulated mind sees all things as they should be seen, appraises them at their proper value, turns them to its own advantage, and adheres firmly to its own opinions, as it knows all their force and weight.[1]

There are laws which if violated will weaken, or prevent the development of, what would otherwise result in a powerful mind. These laws fulfilled and observed prevent weakness, and develop and bring into expression that quality of mind which is recognized as power.

Do not allow anyone to dominate your mind! Many are afraid to express the royalty of their own thoughts and convictions because a friend, neighbor, or relative may disagree or disapprove. This is suppression, or repression, and nothing can grow great or strong under repression. Expression is the law of growth.

The timidity that prohibits you from thinking along forbidden lines of thought always stultifies the mind and prevents it from being clothed with power. Prolonged halting between two opinions prevents the growth of a powerful mind.

Dare to be an explorer in the realm of thought. Dare to think deeply and radically, for the mind, like muscles, grows strong with use.

Greatness lies unborn and unexpressed in the bosom of thousands of men and women because of lack of initiative. The lack of initiative is due to fear. Fear is due to the belief in the reality of two powers: good and bad. And he whose greatness lies unborn in the womb of his soul has a greater belief in the power of evil than in the power of good and because of this fear he does not venture to fulfill the call of his soul and thus obtain the crown of an overcomer and conquerer.

In failing to act, he is already overcome in not daring to act. In

1 The first sentence is from *Uncle Tom's Cabin* by Harriet Beecher Stowe

this sense, fear is the great devil: the foundation and source of all poverty, unhappiness, ill-health, and crime.

Let any human being feel and believe that he can never lack in the possession of any good thing and he is already on the path to prosperity.

Material scientists have discovered that so-called matter cannot be destroyed. Its form may be changed; it can be reduced to invisibility; but, it still exists.

If every ton of inflammable substance were consumed by fire, the planet would weigh exactly the same after as it did before, proving that nothing can be destroyed.[1]

The form is changed, but the matter still exists in other forms.

This itself is evidence that matter is eternal and indestructible. If tons of visible substance can be floated out into the atmosphere and become invisible through the disintegrating power of fire, we know that it must be equally true that the invisible can be made visible. This is being proven today by the great nitrate plants. Through electrical vibration they are condensing and crystalizing the nitrogen of the atmosphere, and it remains for the inventive mind yet to bring out of the atmosphere the foods that we are now taking out of the earth by the process of cultivation.

They who can think far enough and deep enough into the undiscovered realms of knowledge and law as related to electricity and other ethereal forces will be the inventors and discoverers whose names will be written in the Hall of Fame.

Such men must be free from fear; men unmoved and unswerved by ridicule and derision; men who keep their minds fixed and centered upon one great purpose. Such men press on and on, regardless of what others may think or say.

This is initiative, and it is initiative that causes ideals to become real. He who believes that all things are possible, to him all things are possible. Such a believer walks in the path of a Master. The light of inspiration shines upon his path, directs his every step,

1 This is a law of physics, the law of conservation of matter, which states that matter cannot be created nor destroyed.

saves him from pitfalls and stumbling blocks, and leads him triumphantly to the heights of victory.

Nearly every person who has reached mature life has had various manifestations and experiences that reveal to him the fact that there is a mind in him that knows and reveals facts and events that are beyond the possibility of the normal concept or intellectual plane of mind. These manifestations may come in the form of the "still small voice" or a vivid, prophetic dream or vision.

Many times it comes simply as an impression or feeling, especially is this true with the successful business man who acts in accord with the inner voice, or impression, rather than according to appearance or judgments on the external plane, no matter how favorable these judgments may appear to the reasoning mind.

These experiences are the *inner voice* that indicate superior knowledge and wisdom coming to the conscious mind from some mysterious source. It is the same Mind that spoke through all the great masters of ancient or modern times.

This voice and these phenomena come from the third plane of consciousness. It is sometimes called the "sixth sense." In the New Psychology, it is known as *super-consciousness.* This Super Mind knows of your dangers and protects you.

This protection is usually without explanation.

This Super Mind also knows of green pastures and still waters, figures of abundance and peace. It leads the responsive student, who listens in the Silence to its wisdom, and thus he is given opportunities, where without this Counsellor and Guide, he would be overcome with dangers and fruitless efforts and adventures.

Solomon, the greatest financier among the kings of Israel, had this super-consciousness connected with his outer consciousness, thus manifesting efficiently in his private, kingly, and financial affairs, so that he became the wealthiest and most glorious king in the House of Israel.

Sometimes all other avenues of activity or progress become closed to us and then moving into this only open avenue we meet with success, which could have been ours much earlier if we had but known something of the voice of the silence.

When you have established a unity with the Super-conscious Mind, you have with you a revealer, which in a quiet way makes known to you the heart and intent of all persons who come into your presence. The "wolf in sheep's clothing," the Devil in the garb of an angel, and the fox in the garb of a gentle dog are revealed to you in a measure sufficient to put you on guard.

This All-knowing Mind literally becomes a Counsellor, Advocate, and Guide. This inner voice, or intuition, will direct you wisely. It will also warn you and find a way of escape in every time of need.

In order that this may take place, it is important that you should have seasons of solitude, quietness, or silence in which you should allow no interruptions.

Every muscle should be relaxed and the mind withdrawn from all external things and given wholly to a receptive attitude, so that the Super Mind may come forth into manifestation and energize, illumine, and clarify the outer planes of conscious mind.

It is good practice to have a set time or times every day for this silence. You may have other moments of silence, such as a few minutes at your desk, in your parlor, or while riding in the street car or train.

Do not be discouraged if wonderful things do not occur in the Silence. These wonderful things usually occur after the Silence rather than in it.

Do not do the thinking yourself, but let the Infinite One think through you and for you.

At first when thoughts begin to come, they may not be very clear or very correct. Just listen. As the stream of thought flows on, it clarifies itself, and in a few moments you will be receiving wisdom that will help you in your life and work.

If you seem to receive no conscious thought at all, you may be sure that it is being registered on the Subconscious Mind and will be brought forth into the Conscious Mind when needed.

In the silence you become illuminated and inspired and are no longer as experimenter or speculator on the path of life.

In the silence, your experiences will be of a character pertinent to your evolution and unfoldment. Some will catch fertile thoughts and plans; others will have a feeling or impulse to do or not to do the thing they contemplate.

The idea and purpose of the silence is to make connection with the great storehouse of wisdom—to be charged with magnetic vibrations according to your specific need, much the same as charging an electrical storage battery. Thus, when you are low on wisdom, energy, or tact, go into the silence and replenish yourself.

This is charging yourself with power, so that you go back into the business world richly supplied with energy.

It is, thus, that you may go victoriously forward.

There are but few who find the path that really leads to the Holy Grail. It is a secret trail. The entrance is obscured. The careless, shiftless, non-concentrated mind passes it by. They who practice the Silence discover the entrance. They reach their goal.

A razor blade has penetrative power because of it extremely fine edge. It meets with little resistance in passing through and between the molecules of substance. The concentrated mind is one pointed, sharp, and penetrative and finds a way through hard problems; it thus dissolves and disintegrates the seemingly impossible.

Many a perplexed business man has turned the tide of failure into success by devoting a few minutes each day to silent meditation in his place of business. This accomplishes two purposes: It puts him into tune with the Universal Law and places the Law of Attraction into operation, which acts as a magnet in the same manner that honey in the blossom draws the honey bee.

The Silence is the University of the Master Mind. It is here that all wise men have received their wisdom. It is here that the greatest Teacher of all teachers instructs the devotee.

The true silence brings forth the hidden glory, just as the glory of the lily, hidden within the bud, is drawn out by the opening of the bud. So the wisdom and power hidden in man is drawn into expression—or bloom—through self-faith and the use of the silence. This is real education. The word education comes from the Latin word educio, which means "to draw out from within."

If you make it a point to enjoy the silence just as much as you would a visit with a very dear friend, then you will get results much more readily.

The attitude should be one of earnest desire, solicitude, and determination.

To accomplish the greatest result, determine first your greatest desire.

Then concentrate upon that.

Affirm that it can be accomplished.

Affirm that heaven and earth lend you their assistance.

Know that you are not alone, but the indwelling Mind works with you, watches over you, and guides your thought, decisions, and actions.

Relax every muscle; be quiet.

Contemplate the Infinite resources at your command.

Great Captains of Industry have few intimates. They know that great thoughts, great actions, and great achievements are born in the silence.

PART FOUR

The LAW of ATTRACTION

We have discovered that premeditated, orderly thinking for a purpose matures that purpose into fixed form, so that we may be absolutely sure of the result of our dynamic experiment.

—**Francis Larimer Warner**

Attraction is the power that is sweeping through eternity, a living stream of relative action in which the basic principle is ever active. It embraces the past and carries it forward into the ever widening future; a movement where relative action, cause, and effect go hand in hand; where law dovetails into law; and where all laws are the ever willing handmaids of this great creative force.

This power stretches beyond the utmost planets, beyond a beginning, beyond an ending, and on into a beginningless and endless eternity. It causes the things we see to take form and shape. It brings the fruit from the blossom and the sweetness from the honey. It measures the sweep of the countless orbs. It lurks in the sparkle of the diamond, and in the amethyst and the grape. It works in the seen and in the unseen, and it permeates the all.

It is the source of perfect justice, perfect unity, perfect harmony, and perfect truth; while its constant activity brings perfect balance, perfect growth, and perfect understanding.

Perfect justice because it renders equal retribution.

Perfect unity because it has oneness of purpose.

Perfect harmony because in it all laws blend.

Perfect truth because it is the one great truth of all existence.

Perfect balance because it measures unerringly.

Perfect growth because it is a natural growth.

Perfect understanding because it solves every problem of life.

The reality of this law lies in its activity, for only through action and constant change can this law come to be; and only through inaction can it cease to be; but as there is no inaction, there can be no cessation.

The one purpose of this law is unchangeable. In the silence of darkness, in the glory of light, in the turmoil of action and the pain of reaction, it moves ever forward toward the fulfillment of its one great purpose—perfect harmony.

We see and feel its urge in the myriad and myriad of plant forms on hill and in dale as they push forth from the same darkness into one light; and though bathed by the same waters and breathed upon by the same air, yet all varieties maintain their own individuality. That is, the rose is always a rose and differs from the violet, which is always a violet. The acorn gives the world the oak and never a willow or any other variety of tree; and though all send out roots into the same soil and blossom in the same sunshine, yet some are frail, some are strong, some are bitter, and some are sweet; while others are repulsive, some are beautiful. Thus, all varieties draw to themselves through their own roots and from the same elements that which differentiates them from each other. And this great law of life, this constant urge, this hidden force in the plant causing it to manifest, to grow, and to attain, is this Law of Attraction bearing forward in silent majesty bringing all fruition, dictating nothing, yet making each unit of growth true to its own individual nature.

In the mineral world, it is the cohesion of the rock, sand, and clay. It is the strength in the granite, the beauty in the marble, the sparkle in the sapphire, and the blood in the ruby.

Thus do we find it working in the things we see; but its unseen power, as it works in the mind of man, is greater.

This Law of Attraction is neither good nor evil, neither moral nor immoral. It is a neutral law that always flows in conjunction with the desires of the individual. We choose our own line of growth, and there are as many lines of growth as there are individuals; and although no two of us are exactly alike, yet many of us move along similar lines.

These lines of growth are made up of past, present, and future desires manifesting in the ever-forming present, where they establish the central line of our being along which we advance. The nature of these desires has no power to check the action of this, for its function is to bring to maturity the bitter as well as the sweet.

An illustration of the neutrality and action of this law is found in the grafting of an apple tree bud into a wild crab tree, where we find in due time eatable and uneatable fruits growing together on the same tree. That is, wholesome and unwholesome fruits nourished and brought to maturity by the same sap.

In applying this illustration to ourselves, we find that the cultured apples and the wild crabs represent our different desires, while the sap represents this Law of Growth. Just as the sap bring to maturity the different kinds of fruit, just so will this law bring to fruitfulness our different kinds of desires. Whether they be wholesome or unwholesome, it matters not to the law, for its place in life is to bring to our minds a conscious realization of the results that follow all desires we hold, as well as their nature, their effect, and their purpose.

In man's division of the law, we come in contact with a larger activity, one that is utterly unknown to the primitive mind, which leads us to a conscious awakening of a newer power in a larger field of action. In other words, a larger truth, a greater understanding, and a deeper insight.

We are touching a greater reality, for let us understand that reality lies in activity and not outside of it. To exist is to be alive to the action of the laws about us. The hidden urge in the plant is its reality and not the outer form we see.

True knowledge comes to us through our own activities, borrowed knowledge through the activities of others. Both together evolve our intellects. And slowly we are forming a unique self, an individualizing unit.

As we move out into the power of our growing intellects—into an ever-moving consciousness—we are learning to seek for the wherefore and why of things, and in this search we think and imagine that we are original, when in fact we are only students of established beliefs, notions, and facts gathered throughout generations of tribal and national life.

We live in a state of fear and uncertainty until we find and make use of the unvarying uniformity running through all laws. This is the central truth that we must know and use before we can become masters of self, or masters of conditions. The Law of Growth ripens collectively, for its one function is "to act upon that which we give it to act upon."

As the nature of the cause governs the effect, so does the thought precede and predetermine action. Each one must use this law knowingly and consciously; otherwise we use it blindly. Use it we must.

In our growth from primitive man to conscious man, there are three seeming divisions or sections. First, our growth through the savage or unconscious state; second, our growth through the intellectual and conscious growing state; and third, our growth into and conscious recognition of our conscious state.

We all know that the bulb must first send out roots before it can send out shoots, and it must send out shoots before it can come to blossom in the sunlight. It is just so with us. Like the plant, we must first send out roots (our roots are our thoughts) before we can evolve from our primitive or animal bulb-like state into the intellectual and conscious growing state.

Next we, like the plant, must send forth shoots before we can evolve from a purely intellectual state of conscious growing into a conscious state of conscious knowing. Otherwise, we would always remain only creatures of the law and never masters of the law.

Lastly, we, like the plant, must individualize—must come to full bloom. In other words, we must give forth the radiating beauty of a perfected life. We must stand revealed to ourselves and to others as a unit of power and a master over those laws that govern and control our growth. Each has a force within itself and this force is the action of law set into activity by ourselves. It is through this consciousness that we begin to master laws and to bring results through our conscious knowledge of their operation.

Life is a rigid conformity to laws, where we are the conscious or unconscious chemists of our own life. For when life is truly understood, it is found to be made up of chemical action. As we breath in oxygen, chemical action takes place in our blood; as we consume food and water, chemical action takes place in our digestive organs; in our use of thought, chemical action takes place in both mind and body; in the change called death, chemical action takes place and disintegration sets in; so we find that physical existence is chemical action.

Life is made up of laws and as we make use of these laws, so do we get results.

If we think distress, then we get distress; if we think success, then we get success. When we entertain destructive thought, we set up a chemical action that checks digestion, which in turn irritates other organs of the body and reacts upon the mind causing disease and sickness. When we worry, we churn a cesspool of chemical action causing fearful havoc to both mind and body. On the other hand, if we entertain constructive thoughts, we set up a healthy chemical action.

When we entertain negative thoughts, we put into action a poisonous chemical activity of a disintegrating nature that stupefies our sensibilities and deadens our nerve actions, causing the mind and body to become negative and therefore subject to many ills. On the other hand, if we are positive, we put into action a healthy chemical activity of a constructive nature, causing the mind and body to become free from the many ills due to discordant thoughts.

These analyses can be carried through every avenue of life, but enough has been shown to indicate that life is largely chemical action and that the mind is the chemical laboratory of thought, and that we are the chemists in the workshop of mental action where everything is prepared for our use and where the product turned out will be in proportion to the material used. In other words, the nature of the thought we use determines the kinds of conditions and experiences with which we meet. What we put into life we get out of life—no more, no less.

Life is an orderly advancement governed by the Law of Attraction. Our growth is through three seeming sections. In the first, we are creatures of law; in the second, users of law; and in the third, we are masters of law. In the first, we are unconscious users of thought power; in the second, conscious users of thought power; and in the third, we are conscious users of conscious power.

So long as we persist in using only the laws of the first section, we are held in bondage to them. So long as we remain satisfied with the laws and growth of the second section, we shall never become conscious of a greater advancement. In the third section, we awaken to our conscious power over laws of the first and second sections and become fully awake to the laws governing the third.

When rightly understood, life is found not to be a question of chance; not a question of creed; not a question of nationality; not a question of social standing; not a question of wealth; not a question of power. No—all of these have a place to fill in the growth of the individual, but we must all eventually come to know that Harmony comes only as a result of a compliance with Natural Law.

This rigid exactness and stability in the nature of law is our greatest asset, and when we become conscious of this available power and use it judiciously, we shall have found the Truth that will make us free!

Science has of late made such vast discoveries, has revealed such an infinity of resources, has unveiled such enormous possibilities and such unsuspected forces, that scientific men more and more hesitate to affirm certain theories as established and indubitable, or to deny certain other theories as absurd or impossible. And so a new civilization is being born. Customs, creeds, and cruelty are passing; vision, faith, and service are taking their place. The fetters of tradition are being melted from humanity, and as the dross of militarism and materialism are being consumed, thought is being liberated and truth is rising full orbed before an astonished multitude.

We have caught only a glimpse of the possibility of the rule of mind, which means the rule of spirit. We have just begun to realize in a small degree what this newly discovered power may do for us. That it can bring success in this world's affairs is beginning to be understood and practiced by thousands.

The whole world is on the eve of a new consciousness, a new power, and a new realization of resources within the self. The last century saw the most magnificent material progress in history. May the new century produce the greatest progress in mental and spiritual power."

> "Thought is deeper than all speech,
> Feeling deeper than all thought,
> Soul to soul can never teach
> What unto itself is taught."[1]

---

1 Stanza from an early poem by Christopher Pearse Cranch (1813–1892).

PART FIVE

The UNIVERSAL MIND

How to master the thought machinery to meet one's desire is not so difficult as it may appear to be to those unacquainted with true mental discipline. That a man can change himself, improve himself, re-create himself, control his environment, and master his own destiny is the conclusion of every mind who is wide-awake to the power of right thought in constructive action.

—**Larsen**

The nervous system is matter. Its energy is mind. It is therefore the instrument of the Universal Mind. It is the link between matter and spirit—between our consciousness and the Cosmic Consciousness. It is the gateway of Infinite Power.

Both the cerebrospinal and the sympathetic nervous system are controlled by nervous energy that is alike in kind and the two systems are so interwoven that their impulses can be sent from on to the other. Every activity of the body, every impulse of the nervous system, every thought, uses up nervous energy.

The system of nerves may be compared to a telegraph system: the nerve cells corresponding to the batteries, the fibres to the wires. In the batteries is generated electricity. The cells, however, do not generate nervous energy. They transform it and the fibres convey it. This energy is not a physical wave like electricity, light, or sound. It is **mind**.

It bears the same relationship to the mind as a piano does to its player. The Mind can only have perfect expression when the instrument through which it functions is in order.

The organ of the Cerebrospinal Nervous System is the Brain; the organ of the Sympathetic Nervous System is the Solar Plexus. The first is the voluntary of conscious, the latter is the involuntary or the subconscious.

It is through the Cerebrospinal Nervous System and the Brain that we become conscious of possessions, hence all possession has its origin in consciousness. The undeveloped consciousness of a babe or the inhibited consciousness of an idiot cannot posses.

The mental condition—consciousness—increases in direct proportion to our acquisition of knowledge. Knowledge is acquired by observation, experience, and reflection. We become conscious of these possessions by the mind; so that we recognize that possession is based on consciousness; this consciousness we designate the world within. Those possessions of Form that we acquire are of the world without.

That which possesses in the world within is Mind. That which enables us to possess in the world without is also Mind. Mind manifests itself as thoughts, mental pictures, words, and actions.

Thought is therefore creative. Our power to use thought to create the conditions, surroundings, and other experiences of life, depends upon our habit of thinking. What we do depends upon what we are; what we are is the result of what we habitually think. Before we can do, we must be; before we can be, we must control and direct the force of thought within us.

Thought is force. There are but two things in the universe: Force and Form. When we realize that we possess this and direct it and by it act on the forces and forms in the objective world, we shall have made our first experiment in mental chemistry.

The Universal Mind is the "substance" of all force and form, the reality that underlies all. In accordance with fixed laws, from itself and by itself, is all brought into being and sustained. It is the creative power of thought in its perfect expression. The Universal Mind is all consciousness, all power, and is everywhere present. It is essentially the same at every point of its presence—all mind is one mind. This explains the order and harmony of the universe. To comprehend this statement is to possess the ability to understand and solve every problem of life.

Mind has a two-fold expression: conscious or objective, and subconscious and subjective. We come into relationship with the world without by the objective mind; and with the world within by the subconscious mind. Though we are making a distinction between the conscious and subconscious minds, such a distinction does not really exist; but this arrangement will be found convenient. All Mind is One Mind. In all phases of the mental life, there is an indivisible unity and oneness.

The subconscious mind connects us with the Universal Mind and thus we are brought into direct relationship with all power. In the subconscious is stored up the observations and experiences of life that have come to it through the conscious mind. It is the storehouse of memory. The subconscious mind is a great seed plot in which thoughts have been dropped, or experiences conveyed by observation, or happenings planted, to come up again into consciousness with the fruitage of their growth.

Consciousness is the inner, and Thought is the outward expression of power. The two are inseparable. It is impossible to be conscious of a thing without thinking of it.

We have captured the lightening and changed its name to electricity. We have harnessed the waters and made the remorseless flood our servant. By the miracle of thought we have quickened water into vapor to bear the burdens and move the commerce of the world. We have called into being floating palaces that plough the highways of the deep. We have triumphed in our conquest of the air. Although we have moored in the silvern archipelago of the Milky Way, we have conquered time and space.

When two electric wires are in close proximity, the first carrying a heavier load of electricity than the second, the second will receive by induction some current from the first. This will illustrate the attitude of mankind to the Universal Mind. They are not consciously connected with the source of power.

If the second wire were attached to the first, it would become charged with as much electricity as it could carry. When we become conscious of Power, we become a "live wire," because by consciousness we are connected with the Power. In proportion to our ability to use power, we are enabled to meet the various situations that arise in life.

The Universal Mind is the source of all power and all form. We are channels through which this power is being manifested. Consequently, within us is power unlimited, possibilities without end, and all under the control of our own thought. Because we have these powers, because we are in living union with the Universal Mind, we may adjust or control every experience that may come to us.

There are no limitations to the Universal Mind, therefore the better we realize our oneness with this mind, the less conscious will we be of any limitation or lack, and the more conscious of power.

The Universal Mind is the same at every point of its presence, whether in the infinitely large or the infinitely small. The difference in the power relatively manifested lies in the ability of expression. A stick of clay and a stick of dynamite of equal weight contain much the same amount of energy. But in the one, it is readily set free, whereas in the other we have not yet learned how to release it.

In order to express, we must create the corresponding condition in our consciousness. Either in the Silence or by repetition we impress this condition upon the subconscious.

Consciousness apprehends and Thought manifests the conditions desired. Conditions in our life and in our environment are but the reflection of our predominant thoughts. So the importance of correct thinking cannot be overestimated. "Having eyes and seeing not, having ears and hearing not, neither do they understand," is another way of expressing the truth that without consciousness there can be no apprehension.

Thought constructively used creates tendencies in the subconsciousness. These tendencies manifest themselves as character. The primary meaning of the word "character" is an engraved mark, as on a seal, and means, "the peculiar qualities impressed by nature or habit on a person, which separates the person possessing them from all others." Character has an outward and an inward expression. The inward being purpose, and the outward ability.

Purpose directs the mind towards the ideal to be realized, the object to be accomplished, or the desire to be materialized. Purpose gives quality to thought. Ability is the capacity to cooperate with Omnipotence, although this may be done unconsciously. Our purpose and our ability determine our experiences in life. It is important that purpose and ability be balanced. When the former is greater than the latter, the "Dreamer" is produced; when ability is greater than purpose, impetuosity is the result, producing much useless activity.

By the Law of Attraction, our experiences depend upon our mental attitude. Like is attracted to like. Mental attitude is as much the result of character as character is of mental attitude. Each acts and reacts on the other.

"Chance," "Fate," "Luck," and "Destiny" seem to be blind influences at work behind every experience. This is not so, but every experience is governed by immutable laws, which may be controlled so as to produce the conditions that we desire.

Everything visible and tangible in the universe is composed of matter, which is acted upon by force. As a matter is known to us by its external appearances, we shall designate it as form.

Form may be divided into four classes. That possessing Form only, or the inorganic, as for example iron or marble. Form that is living, or the organic, as for example plants and the vegetable world in general. Form that has both sensation and voluntary motion, as in animals. Form that in addition to sensation and voluntary motion is conscious of its own being and its possessions, as man.

The fundamental principle underlying every successful business relation or social condition is the recognition of the difference between the world within and the world without, the subjective world and the objective world.

Around you, as the center of it, the world without revolves. Matter, organized life, people, thoughts, sounds, light and other vibrations, the universe itself with its numberless millions of phenomena; all sending out vibrations toward you, vibrations of light, of sound, of touch; loudness, softness; of love, hate, of thoughts good and bad, wise and unwise, true and untrue. These vibrations are directed toward you—your ego—by the smallest, as well as by the greatest, the farthest, and the nearest. A few of them reach your world within, but the rest pass by, and as far as you are immediately concerned, are lost.

Some of these vibrations, or forces, are essential to your health, your power, your success, your happiness. How is it that they have passed you by and have not been received in your world within?

Luther Burbank[1] says: "We are just beginning to realize what a wonderful machine is the human brain. We are at the threshold of knowledge, but until yesterday we were outside. The human race has been broadcasting and receiving, perhaps millions of years, without knowing, but suffering all the while from bad thoughts received, and inflicting suffering by bad thoughts sent. The radio, while but a very simple instrument as compared with the brain, is

1 Luther Burbank (1849-1926) was a widely known botanist and scientist who earned fame in breeding new fruits, plants, and flowers. He was also an iconoclast and free-thinker.

helping us to understand what the brain is capable of doing—and is doing.

"Those who are familiar with the radio know what jamming means—the crowding into a narrow wave-belt of a great many sending stations, all operating at once. Since we are all transmitting every time we think, it is obvious that the jamming in wave-length belts used by radio transmitters is as nothing compared with the din made by a billion and a half human brains. Din may seem to be a strange word to use in connection with the ether over a quiet meadow, for instance, but those who know how to operate radio receiving sets will understand. No matter how much jamming is going on, a radio receiving set is as quiet as the grave until it is adjusted and made resonant by establishing harmony within it. The silence may change into what may seem to be almost screaming.

"With everybody broadcasting at once, it follows that the ether must be the sounding chamber into which is crowded every kind of human thought. As we do not broadcast with the same intensity, it follows that the weaker vibrations must be drowned out by the stronger ones. Weak thoughts must soon fall flat, while strong ones may go to the ends of the earth for aught anyone knows. But it seems logical to believe that thoughts, held in common by millions may, because of their identical nature, swell into tremendous chorus, even though the human transmitters may not individually be very strong senders."

Considering consciousness as a general term, we may say that it is the action of the objective upon the subjective. This takes place continuously whether we are awake or asleep. Consciousness is the result of sensing or feeling.

We easily recognize three phases of consciousness, between each of which there are enormous differences.

1. **Simple consciousness**, which all animals possess in common. It is the sense of existence by which we recognize that "we are," and "that we are where we are," and by which we perceive the various objects and varied scenes and conditions.

2. **Self consciousness**, possessed by all mankind, except in-

fants and the mentally deficient. This gives us the power of self-contemplation, i.e., the effect of the world without upon our world within. "Self contemplates self." Amongst many other results, language has thus come into existence, each word being a symbol for a thought or an idea.

3. **Cosmic consciousness**, this form of consciousness is as much above self-consciousness as self-consciousness is above simple consciousness. It is as different from either as sight is different from hearing or touch. A blind man can get no true notion of color, however keen his hearing or sensitive his touch.

Neither by simple consciousness nor by self consciousness can one get any notion of cosmic consciousness. It is not like either of them any more than sight is like hearing. A deaf man can never learn of the value of music by means of his senses of sight or of touch.

Cosmic consciousness is all forms of consciousness. It overrides time and space, for apart from the body and the world of matter, these do not exist.

The immutable law of consciousness is that in the degree that the consciousness is developed, so is the development of power in the subjective and its consequent manifestation in the objective.

Cosmic consciousness is the result of the creation of the necessary conditions, so that the Universal Mind may function in the direction desired. All vibrations in harmony with the Ego's well-being are caught and used.

When the truth is directly apprehended, or becomes a part of consciousness, without the usual process of reasoning or observation, it is intuition. By intuition, the mind instantly perceives the agreement or the disagreement between two ideas. The Ego always so recognizes truth.

By intuition the mind transforms knowledge into wisdom, experience into success, and takes into the world within the things that have been waiting for us in the world without. Intuition, then, is another phase of the Universal Mind that presents truth as facts of consciousness.

PART SIX

The CONSCIOUS MIND

The CONSCIOUS MIND

All the lost mines of Mexico, all the argosies that ever sailed from the Indies, all the gold and silver-laden ships of the treasure fleets stored in Spain count no more in value than a beggar's dole compared to the wealth that is created every eight hours by modern business ideas.

Opportunity follows perception, action follows inspiration, growth follows knowledge, environment follows progress; always the mental first, then the transformation into the illimitable possibilities of character and achievement.

The progress of the United States is due to two percent of its population. In other words, all our railroads, all our telephones, our automobiles, our libraries, our newspapers, and a thousand other conveniences, comforts, and necessities are due to the creative genius of two percent of the population.

As a natural consequence, the same two percent are the millionaires of our country. Now, who are these millionaires, these creative geniuses, these men of ability and energy, to whom we owe practically all the benefits of civilization?

Thirty percent of them were sons of poor preachers who had never earned more than $1,500 a year; twenty-five percent were the sons of teachers, doctors, and country lawyers; and only five percent were the sons of bankers.

We are interested, therefore, in ascertaining why the two percent succeeded in acquiring all that is best in life and the ninety-eight percent remain in perpetual want. We know that this is not a matter of chance because the universe is governed by law. Law governs solar systems, sun, stars, planets. Law governs every form of light, heat, sound, and energy. Law governs every material thing and every immaterial thought. Law covers the earth with beauty and fills it with bounty. Shall we then not be certain that it also governs the distribution of this bounty?

Financial affairs are governed by law just as surely, just as positively, just as definitely as health, growth, harmony, or any other condition of life, and the law is one with which anyone can comply.

Many are already unconsciously complying with this law; others are consciously coming into harmony with it.

Compliance with the law means joining the ranks of the two percent. In fact, the new era, the golden age, the industrial emancipation, means that the two percent is about to expand until the prevailing conditions shall have been reversed—the two percent will soon become the ninety-eight percent.

In seeking the truth we are seeking ultimate cause. We know that every human experience is an effect; therefore, if we may ascertain the cause, and if we shall find that this cause is one that we can consciously control, the effect or the experience will be within our control also.

Human experience will then no longer be the football of fate; a man will not be the child of fortune; but destiny, fate, and fortune will be controlled as readily as a captain controls a vessel or an engineer his train.

All things are finally resolvable into the same thing, and as they are thus translatable, one thing into the other, they must ever be in relation and may never be in opposition to one another.

In the physical world there are innumerable contrasts and these may, for the sake of convenience, be designated by distinctive names. There are surfaces, colors, shades, dimensions, or ends to all things. There is a North Pole and a South Pole; and inside and an outside; a seen and an unseen; but these expressions merely serve to place extremes in contrast.

They are names given to two different parts or aspects of the same quantity. The two extremes are relative; they are not separate entities, but are two parts or aspects of one whole.

In the mental world we find the same law. We speak of knowledge and ignorance, but ignorance is but a lack of knowledge and is therefore found to be simply a word to express the absence of knowledge. It has no principle of itself.

In the moral world we speak of good and evil, but upon investigation, we find that good and evil are but relative terms. Thought precedes and predetermines action; if this action results in benefit to ourselves and others, we call this result good. If this result is to the disadvantage of ourselves and others, we call it evil. Good and evil are therefore found to be simply words that have been coined to indicate the result of our actions, which in turn are the result of our thoughts.

In the Industrial World, we speak of Labor and Capital as if there were two separate and distinct classes, but Capital is wealth and wealth is a product of Labor, and Labor necessarily includes Industry of every kind—physical, mental, executive, and professional. Every man or woman who depends in whole or in part for his or her income upon the results of his or her effort in the Industrial World must be classed as Labor. We therefore find that in the Industrial World there is but one Principle and that is Labor, or Industry.

There are many who are seriously and earnestly trying to find the solution to the present industrial and social chaos, and we hear much of production, waste, efficiency, and sometimes something in regard to constructive thinking.

The thought that humanity is on the borderland of a new idea, that the dawn of a new era is at hand, that a new epoch in the history of the world is about to take place, is rapidly spreading from mind to mind and is changing the preconceived ideas of man and his relation to Industry.

We know that every condition is the result of a cause and that the same cause invariably produces the same result. What has been the cause of similar changes in the thought of the world, such as the Renaissance, the Reformation, the Industrial Revolution? Always the discovery and discussion of new knowledge.

The elimination of competition by the centralization of industry into corporations and trusts and the economies resulting therefrom have set man to thinking.

He sees that competition is not necessary to progress and he is asking, "What will be the outcome of the evolution that is taking place in the Industrial World?" And gradually the thought begins to dawn, the thought that is rapidly germinating, that is about to burst forth in the minds of all men everywhere, the thought that is carrying men off their feet and crowding out every selfish idea, the thought that the emancipation of the Industrial World is at hand.

This is the thought that is arousing the enthusiasm of mankind as never before. This is the thought that is centralizing force and energy and which will destroy every barrier between itself and purpose. It is not a vision of the future; it is a vision of the present; it is at the door—and the door is open.

The creative instinct in the individual is his spiritual nature. It is a reflection of the Universal Creative Principle. It is therefore instinctive and innate. It cannot be eradicated. It can only be perverted.

Owing to the changes that have taken place in the Industrial World, this creative instinct no longer finds expression. A man cannot build his own house; he can no longer make his own garden; he can by no manner of means direct his own labor; he is therefore deprived of the greatest joy that can come to the individual, the joy of creating achievement. And so this great power for good is perverted and turned into destructive channels. Becoming envious, he attempts to destroy the works of his more fortunate fellows.

Thought results in action. If we wish to change the nature of the action, we must change the thought, and the only way to change the thought is to substitute a healthy mental attitude for the chaotic mental conditions existing at present.

It is evident that the power of thought is by far the greatest power in existence. It is the power that controls every other power and while this knowledge has until recently been the possession of the few, it is about to become the priceless privilege of the many. Those who have the imagination—the vision—will see the opportunity of directing this thought into constructive and creative channels. They will encourage and foster the spirit of mental adventure. They will arouse, develop, and direct the creative instinct, in which case we shall soon see such an industrial revival as the world has never before experienced.

Henry Ford visions the approach of the new era in *The Dearborn Independent*. He says:

> The human race is now on the borderline between two periods: the period when to use is to lose, and

the period when not to use is to waste. For a long time, mankind has been conscious of somehow coming to the end of irresponsible childhood; the provision made by the Parent of mankind has seemed to be coming to the end of its lavishness. That is, there has been a sense that the more we used the less we had in reserve. This feeling has been expressed in the popular adage, "You can't eat your cake and have it."

But now that man is learning enough to plant his supply as well as reap it, to make his supply a recurrent crop instead of a slowly diminishing original store of natural resources, the time is coming when instead of being afraid of wasting our resources by using them we shall be afraid of wasting them by not using them. The stream of supply will be so full and constant that when people worry it will not be worry about not having enough, but about not using enough.

If you can imagine a world in which the source of supply will be so plentiful that people will worry about not using enough of it, instead of worrying as we do now about using too much, you will have a picture of the world that is soon to be. We have long depended on the resources which nature long ago stored up, the resources which can be exhausted. We are entering an era when we shall create resources which shall be so constantly renewed that the only loss will be not to use them. There will be such a plenteous supply of heat, light, and power, that it will be sin not to use all we want. This era is coming in now. And it is coming by way of water.

With the fuel question settled, and the light question settled, and the heating question settled, and the power question settled, on such terms as actually liberate the whole world from the crushing weight of these four great burdens; and not only that, but with the whole fuel and light and heat and

> power situation turned around so that people will have to use all that they want, in order to prevent waste—don't you see how economic life will swing loose and breathe deeply, as if a new spring day had dawned for humanity?
>
> That is the era we are approaching. There is no question about that. There will be, of course, the usual preliminary skirmish between selfishness and service, but service will win. The ownership of a coal mine located on a man's property may easily be granted to private parties, but the ownership of a river! Nature itself rebukes the man who would claim ownership of a river.
>
> Our next period is before us, not the first period of reckless waste, nor the second period of anxious accounting, but the third period of overlapping abundance which compels us to use and use and use, to fulfill every need.

Thought is mind in motion, just as wind is air in motion. Mind is a spiritual activity; in fact, it is the only activity that the spiritual man possesses, and Spirit is the creative Principle of the Universe.

Therefore, when we think, we start a train of causation. The thoughts go forth and meet other similar thoughts; they coalesce and form ideas; the ideas now exist independently of the thinker; they are the invisible seeds which exist everywhere, and which sprout and grow and bring forth fruit, some a hundredfold and some a thousandfold.

We have been led to believe, and many still seem to think, that Wealth is something very material and tangible—that we can secure and hold it for our own exclusive use and benefit. We somehow forget that all the gold in the world only amounts to a very few dollars per capita. The entire supply of gold for the world is only eight billion dollars.

This includes all the gold coined or in bars in the various banks or government treasuries of the world. This quantity of gold could be easily contained in a sixty-foot cube. If we depended upon the supply of gold it would be exhausted in a single day, and yet with this as a basis we spend hundreds and thousands, millions and now billions, of dollars daily, and yet the original supply of gold is not altered. The gold is simply a measure, a rule. With one ruler we may measure thousands and hundreds of thousands of feet, so with one five dollar bill hundreds and thousands and millions of people may have the use of it by simply passing it from one to the other.

So it is that if we can only keep the tokens of wealth, which we call money, circulating, everyone could have all he or she might want; there need be no lack. The sense of lack comes only when we begin to hoard, when we are seized with fear and panic and fail to give out, to release.

It is therefore evident that the only way we can get any benefit from wealth is by its use and to use it we must give it out so that someone else can get the benefit of it. We are then cooperating for our mutual benefit and putting the law of abundance into practical operation.

We also see that wealth is by no means as substantial and tangible as many suppose, but that, on the contrary, the only way to get it is to keep it going. As soon as there is any concerted movement whereby there is any danger of stopping the circulation of this medium of exchange there is stagnation, fever, panic, and industrial death.

It is this intangible nature of wealth that makes it peculiarly susceptible to the power of thought and has enabled many men to secure fortunes in a year or two which others could not hope to acquire in a lifetime of effort. This is due to the creative power of mind.

Helen Wilmans[1] gives an interesting description of the practical operation of this law in *The Conquest of Poverty*. She says:

> There is an almost universal reaching out for money. This reaching out is from the acquisitive fac-

---

1 Helen Wilmans (1831-1907) was a Florida faith healer who wrote many books about the "mental science" including *Lessons in Mental Science* and *Second Birth: A Practical Treatise on Mental Healing*.

ulties only and its operations are confined to the competitive realm of the business world. It is a purely external proceeding; its mode of action is not rooted in the knowledge of the inner life, with its finer, more just, and spiritualized wants. It is but an extension of animality into the realm of the human, and no power can lift it to the divine plane the race is now approaching.

For all lifting on this plane is the result of spiritual growth. It is doing just what Christ said we must do in order to be rich. It is first seeking the kingdom or heaven within, where alone it exists. After this kingdom is discovered, then all these things (external wealth) shall be added.

What is there within a man that can be called the kingdom of heaven? When I answer this question not one reader out of ten will believe me, so utterly bankrupt of knowledge of their own internal wealth are the great majority of people. But I shall answer it, nevertheless, and it will be answered truly.

Heaven exists within us in the faculties latent in the human brain, the superabundance of which no man has ever dreamed. The weakest man living has the powers of a God folded within his organization; and they will remain folded until he learns to believe in their existence, and then tries to develop them. Men generally are not introspective, and this is why they are not rich. They are poverty-stricken in their own opinions of themselves and their powers, and they put the stamp of their belief on everything they come in contact with. If a day laborer, let us say, does but look within himself long enough to perceive that he has an intellect that can be made as great and far reaching as that of the man he serves; if he sees this, and attaches due importance to it, the mere fact of his seeing it has, to a degree, loosened his bonds and brought him face to face with better conditions.

But there is wanted something more than the fact of knowing that he is, or may become, by recognition of self, his employer's intellectual equal. There remains the fact that he needs also to know the Law and claim its provisions; namely, that his superior knowing relates him to a superior position. He must know this and trust it; for it is by holding this truth in faith and trust that he begins to ascend bodily. Employers everywhere hail with delight the acquisitions of employees who are not machines—they want brains in their business and are glad to pay for them. Cheap help is often the most expensive, in the sense of being the least profitable. As brain growth or development of thought power in the employee increases his value to his employer, and as the employee grows to the degree of strength where he is capable of doing for himself, there will be another not yet grown so strong to take his place.

The gradual recognition by a man of his own latent powers is the heaven within that is to be brought forward in the world and established in these conditions which correlate it.

A mental poor-house projects from itself the spirit of a visible poor-house, and this spirit expresses itself in visible externals correlated to its character.

A mental palace sends forth the spirit of a visible palace with results that correlate it. And the same may be said of sickness and sin, of health and goodness.

PART SEVEN

The CREATIVE PROCESS

There is nothing truer than that the quality of thought which we entertain correlates certain externals in the outside world. This is the Law from which there is no escape. And it is this Law, this correlative of the thought with its object, that from time immemorial has led the people to believe in special providence.

—Williams

If the chemist produces nothing of value, nothing which can be converted into cash, we are not interested. But, fortunately, the chemist in this case produces an article that has the highest cash value of any article known to man.

He provides the one thing which all the world demands, something which can be realized upon anywhere, at any time. It is not a slow asset; on the contrary, its value is recognized in every market.

The product is thought; thought rules the world; thought rules every government, every bank, every industry, every person and every thing in existence, and is differentiated from everything else, simply and only because of thought.

Every person is what he is because of his method of thinking, and men and nations differ form each other only because they think differently.

What then is *thought*? Thought is the product of the chemical laboratory possessed by every thinking individual. It is the blossom, the combined intelligence that is the result of all previous thinking processes. It is the fruit and contains the best of all that the individual has to give.

There is nothing material about a thought, and yet no man would give up his ability to think for all the gold in Christendom. It is therefore of more value than anything which exists. As it is not material it must be spiritual. Here then is an explanation of the wonderful value of thought. Thought is a spiritual activity. In fact, it is the only activity which the spirit possesses. Spirit is the creative principle of the Universe. As a part must be the same in kind and quality as the whole, and can differ only in degree, thought must be creative also.

The ancients felt that every piece of sculpture was the embodiment of an idea or sentiment and was produced on the principle that there is a perfect correspondence between mental states and physical expression.

We of the present day recognize that there is a direct correspondence between mental states and the condition of the human body, and that knowledge has been so formulated that we now know that every condition is an effect and this effect is a result of a cause that had its origin in an idea.

Modern science is now directing attention to the fact that ideas are also responsible for every form of wealth and its distribution. The science of economics is therefore seen to be the science that treats of the laws governing ideas and there expression on a material plane.

It takes the sun about two thousand years to pass from one sign of the Zodiac[1] to another. In Oriental literature, these are called "sub-race periods," for it is during such a period that a nation is born, matures, grows old, and dies. Most of the European nations are now ending their two thousand year cycle and the necessary readjustments are taking place. It remains then for us, a new nation, in a new world, to assist in the readjustment.

In this readjustment it might be well to remember that intelligence rules; that constructive thought intelligently directed automatically causes its object to materialize on the objective plane; that cause and effect are supreme in a universe governed by immutable law; that it is the mind alone which can furnish the knowledge with which to ameliorate the conditions of life. It is the mind that builds every house, writes every book, paints every picture; it is the mind that suffers and enjoys; it follows then that a knowledge of the functions of the mind ranks first in importance to the human race.

Senator Wadsworth[2] recently said: "I pray that the time will come when American public opinion will come to an appreciation of what organic chemistry means in the way of progress. We have been interested as a people in the development of material resources—the digging of iron and coal from the ground, the raising of crops upon the surface, and the engaging in transportation, and other forms of commercial effort. As a people, we have paid little attention and given little encouragement to scientific research, but Mr. President and Senators, the progress of the future depends

1 To learn much more about the Zodiac, read Haanel's *A Book About You*.
2 James Wolcott Wadsworth,Jr. (1877-1952) became a US Senator in 1915.

upon scientific research. It is the man working in the chemical laboratory who is to blaze the way for human progress."

He went on to say: "I believe that in organic chemistry lies the solution of the secrets of the past and of the future. I believe that its establishment and maintenance in this country, even under an embargo, means the happiness, the progress, and the security of 100,000,000 people."

Senator Frelinghuysen[1] added: "When we realize that it was due to the genius of the German chemists and the advance in the science by the German industries that enabled Germany to get almost to the channel ports; when we realize that the next war will be fought with chemicals, I think it is our patriotic duty to give this industry the highest protection that can be imposed."

It is true that many of the more important discoveries in science are due to the genius of German chemists. It is also true that the next war, if there be one, will be fought with chemicals. But the next and all future wars will be won by an understanding of mental chemistry.

Try to realize the situation. Think for a moment. See an army of men pass in review, four abreast, all men in the prime of life. See them march on and on. Men from Germany, men from France, from England, from Belgium, from Austria, from Russia, from Poland, from Rumania, from Bulgaria, from Servia, from Turkey, yes and from China and Japan, India, New Zealand, Australia, Egypt, and America. On they go, marching all day long, all the next day and the day after, all the week they keep coming and the next week and the next week and the next month, for it would take months for this army of ten million men to pass any given point. All dead, and dead only because a few men in high places were more concerned about organic chemistry than they were about mental chemistry. They did not know that force can always be met with equal or su-

1 Theodore Frelinghuysen (1787–1862) was New Jersey's Attorney General, a US Senator, and Mayor of Newark, NJ before running for Vice-President with Henry Clay in 1844. He led the opposition to the Indian Removal Act of 1830, about which he said, "Let us beware how, by oppressive encroachments upon the sacred privileges of our Indian neighbors, we minister to the agonies of future remorse."

perior force. They did not know that a higher law always controls a lower law. And because intelligent men and women allowed a few men in high places to control their thinking processes, the entire world must sit in sack-cloth and ashes, for the living will find it necessary to work the rest of their lives in order to even pay the interest on the obligations assumed, and their children will find these obligations an inheritance, and they in turn will pass them on to their children and their children's children.

A celebrated European statesman visions the present situation as follows:

"Unfortunately, the ills of a war like that of 1914-1918 are repaired but with difficulty. Given even the entire good faith of the conquered, if the latter by conscientious labor genuinely desired to help the world out of its sanguinary nightmare and back to normal life, that world would none the less remain for a long time hopelessly adrift and at sea. We are assisting today at the prolongation of a war which is not even likely to approach a conclusion unless there is a new orientation of a peace-time energy. Finances upside down, budgets artificially met, rates of exchange giving 65 francs to the pound and 14 to the dollar, a terribly distorted fiduciary circulation, an ever-increasing cost of living, strikes, rapid changes in the stock markets making commerce and industry impossible, accumulation of stocks—such is the ransom of these four years of war. It was materially impossible that either for conqueror or conquered aught else should result from this world catastrophe than complete chaos for all. Millions of men are not consecrated for 52 months to a work of death and destruction for the world to be re-established on the morrow of peace. Such rapidly reacquired equilibrium is beyond the bounds of human practicability."

It will be remembered that the Master Metaphysician said the same thing in somewhat different language many years ago:

> Then shall be great tribulation such as never was since the beginning of the world, nor never shall be afterwards, and if that period would not be shortened no flesh at all would be saved, but for the elect's sake that period will be shortened.
>
> —Matthew 24:21,22

That people are beginning to think is evident. Formerly, when men were discontented or dissatisfied, they met in a near-by saloon, had a few drinks, and promptly forgot their discontent and dissatisfaction. The situation is very different under existing conditions. Men spend their time reading, studying, and thinking, and the more they think the less satisfied they become.

Leaders of men all know this. For this reason, England has her ale, Scotland her whiskey, France her absinthe, Germany her beer, and we of America, who are recruited from all of these have had all forms of alcohol. It is by far the easiest way of keeping the people "happy and contented." A man who has access to a fair percentage of alcohol will not ask too many questions. If he does, give him another drink.

This method of reducing the citizens of a country to a kind of idiotic servility has the additional advantage in that it produces enormous revenues that may be used for reducing them to economic slavery as well as spiritual slavery, for the man who cannot think has but small prospect of ever coming into any understanding of spiritual truth.

The history of the world confirms this conclusion. Egypt, once at the head of nations, has, under the weight of her own effeminacy, gone down to the dust. The victories of Greece let in upon her glory with a night of ages. And Rome, whose iron foot trod down the nations and shook the earth, witnessed in her latter days faintness of heart and the shield of the mighty vilely cast away.

Ten years ago, the securities of German corporations sold side by side with those of England and America. No one dreamed that they were not absolutely safe. The municipal bonds of any large German city sold freely on a 4 percent basis in London, Paris, and New York. The mark was as stable as the dollar or pound sterling.

The interest is still being paid upon these securities and the principal will be paid at maturity, but in money that is hardly worth the paper it is printed upon, and so the conservative German investor, the man who made only "safe" investments, who was careful to buy only first mortgage bonds that yielded not more than 4 or 5 percent, is practically penniless; but as a compensation he can reflect that a liberal government allowed the people to have plenty of beer, and when men have plenty of beer they will unlikely be glad to let some one else do the thinking for them. For the use of beer is not calculated to produce deep, clear, sustained, or logical thought.

Thousands and tens of thousands of American citizens are slowly and painfully creating a fund that they hope will protect them in the days to come. Is it possible that they, too, will be paid in valueless dollars ten years from now?

The reason that the dollar will probably remain at par is because we do not desire the kind of personal liberty that enriches a few at the expense of the many, the kind of liberty that attempts to reduce American citizens to automatons in order that a few may dictate the destiny of the nation.

We of America must remember that the large business of life is not economically conducted unless we succeed in transforming our resources into the highest grade of physical, mental, and moral persons evolvable.

Marion Leroy Burton, President of the University of Michigan, says: "Perhaps the most solemn question that can be put to a person today is, 'Can you think?' The test of individual efficiency and usefulness to society centers in a man's ability to use his mind. Emerson never erected a more arresting danger signal when he exclaimed, 'Beware when the great God lets loose a thinker on the planet.' If we could only harness the mental power of America today we could solve the gigantic problems of the world. Not by appeals to prejudice and class interest, not by the hurling of epithets, not by the ready acceptance of half truths, not by superficial, but by careful painstaking, scientific, scholarly thought combined with wise and timely action, will civilization be rescued and human freedom made secure. Upon education depends the future of democracy. Therefore, loyal citizen, Every self-respecting person must utilize his opportunities to strengthen his grip on knowledge and to stimulate his mind. The truth has always made men free, and truth is available only for him who thinks."

Roger W. Babson[1] says:

---

1 Roger W. Babson (1875-1967) was a statistician and columnist who said, among other things, "It takes a person who is wide awake to make his dream come true."

> If statistics have taught us any one thing during the past twenty years, it is that the spiritual factor is the greatest factor in the growth of communities and nations. It is well enough to talk about land, labor, and capital. They all have their uses and functions, but of themselves they are helpless in bringing about prosperity. Land, labor, and capital existed long before there was even civilization. Many great nations, such as Babylon, Persia, Egypt, Greece, Rome, and even Spain, have possessed land, labor, and capital in abundance, but fell for want of this far more important quality—the spiritual factor.
>
> I'm looking out of my window at the highway where a man is at work with a pick. The highway is the land; the man is the labor; and the pick is the capital. This is a perfect illustration of land, labor, and capital; but it also illustrates that such a combination can be used either to destroy or to construct—to break up the road or to repair the road. The man can use the pick to make the ruts and holes deeper or to fill them up. It all depends upon the purpose, the motive, and the desire of man. Purpose, motive, and desire are spiritual factors and are all important. Land, labor, and capital, and even education, are mere tools that can be used either for good or for evil. Two men graduate from the same law school and get the same degree; one uses his education to uphold the law and the other uses his education to help men evade the law. Two chemists graduate from the same technical school in the same class; one uses his training to make foods pure and the other uses the same training to adulterate foods.

Thinking is a creative process and combination is the key. Nature combines electrons, atoms, molecules, cells, and the final result is the Universe. In the field of human endeavor, all progression, development, and achievement is the result of following the lesson learned from nature, and man has risen step by step from the primitive brute state to his present position of mastership by combining, uniting, and relating thoughts, things, and forces.

In the domain of science and invention, in the realm of art, literature, and business, in every department of human activity, by combining the common, the usual, the known, man has unveiled and discovered the uncommon, the unusual, the unknown. Man has progressed rapidly in spite of the fact that the method pursued in finding out new combinations was used unconsciously and unsystematically. In order to eliminate accident and chance, there must be employed a scientific method applied consciously and systematically, exhaustively, earnestly, honestly, continuously, resulting in greater success, more wonderful discoveries, more numerous and astounding inventions.

Every time we breathe, we take into our lungs not only air, but spirit or *prana*[1], the breath of life.

Every element in the material world is in every breath we take. From these elements, the cabbage takes what it wants to form cabbage. From these same elements, the apple tree forms and colors an apple; and the rose from these elements produces, colors, and perfumes a rose. Surely it was intended that man should know as much as the cabbage, the apple, or the rose about handling these elements.

There is one universal substance out of which all things are formed and the difference between flesh, vegetable, stone, iron, and glass is the difference in the vibration or motion of these particles of substance as they are brought together and act and react upon one another.

Form is the expression of Spirit, Mind, Life, and Energy. The human brain is the finest, most vibrant vehicle on this plane of existence, and thus it has power to control all things. When we think or concentrate along any particular line, we start a train of causation, and if our thought is sufficiently concentrated and kept continuously in mind, what happens?

There is only one thing that can happen. Whatever the vision we have, the imagination we have, the image is accepted by the

1 For more about *prana*, read Haanel's *The Amazing Secrets of the Yogi*.

Universal Intelligence expressing through the cells of our physical body and environment and these cells send out their calls into the great formless energy for the material that corresponds with the image and harmonizes in its vibration with it. If the image is for success along any particular line or fear of a particular thing, we call the atoms from out of the formless energy which make for the success or the thing we fear—and thus we relate with conditions according to the energy created through the instrumentality of the human mind.

Thought acts upon the body or environment subconsciously. *The New York Times* tells how the same result is being accomplished by the government by the use of mechanical means. The subject of the article is "How Skill is Gained in Sleep."

"Wise folk will refrain from expressing either amusement or incredulity when they read about the discovery at the government station near Pensacola that students in the radio school conducted there are gaining speed otherwise unattainable in the receiving of code radio from rapidly transmitted messages heard by them through instruments strapped to their ears when they go to bed. Why the expectation of getting the message does not keep them awake is a little mysterious, but go to sleep they do before taking these strange lessons, and discoveries made in the last twenty years in the domain of the unconscious or subconscious are sufficient to account for the possibility if teaching in this way. After all, whether it can be done or not is a matter of fact to be determined by experience.

"According to the officials at the station, the thing has been done and now has become a routine procedure.

"The subconscious part of the brain possesses many remarkable abilities, some of which long have been known, though unrecognized for what they are, while others are coming to light almost daily as the investigations of the psychologists go on. Not a few familiar activities are performed really well only after we have ceased to do them by conscious effort. The skilled typist leaves the finding of the keys entirely as it seems to her fingers, and the piano player does the same thing. The driver of a motor car who has to think what to do when an emergency arises is a dangerous person to ride with; to be safe he must do the right thing 'automatically,' it used to be said, but now his efficiency is ascribed to the training which his subconscious has received.

"As the subconscious never sleeps and never forgets, the teaching it receives has lasting effects, and there is no reason why such teaching should not be direct and intentional rather than indirect and unintentional, or at least unrealized, as it has been in the past.

"If radio operators can attain by practice in receiving code messages while asleep a skill that is beyond their reach when all their practicing is done while awake, it seems more than probably that instruction for other purposes can be given in the same way. Thence the humorist presumably will imagine and describe schools and colleges where both teachers and pupils do all their mental labor after they have gone to bed and put the lights out. The fact, however, that a theory can be reduced to an absurdity by pushing it to its logical extremity does not prove the theory unsound when its application is kept within reasonable bounds.

"Anybody who under expert guidance makes a list of the number of tasks he daily entrusts with entire confidence to his subconscious powers will be surprised at their number. They begin with the beating of the heart and the drawing of the breath and they go on to decide as to which hand shall be extended for shaking when we meet a friend and into which pocket we shall reach to get a knife or a pencil.

"The difference between ability and inability to swim is a mystery to the conscious mind, for no swimmer can tell what he does after he learns that is different from what he did before that art was gained. But the subconscious knows and makes an easy job of what a little before was an impossibility."

PART EIGHT

VIBRATION

We may divide thinkers into those who think for themselves and those who think through others. The latter are the rule and the former the exception. The first are original thinkers in a double sense, and egoists in the noble meaning of the word. It is from them only that the world learns wisdom. For only the light which we have kindled in ourselves can illuminate others.

—**Schopenhauer**

Before any environment, harmonious or otherwise, can be created, action of some kind is necessary, and before any action is possible, there must be thought of some kind, either conscious or unconscious, and as thought is a product of mind, it becomes evident that Mind is the creative center from which all activities proceed.

It is not expected that any of the inherent laws that govern the modern business world as it is at present constituted can be suspended or repealed by any force on the same plane, but it is axiomatic that a higher law may overcome a lower one. Tree life causes the sap to ascend, not by repealing the law of gravity, but by surmounting it.

The naturalist who spends much of his time in observing visible phenomena is constantly creating power in that portion of his brain set apart for observation. The result is that he becomes very much more expert and skillful in knowing what he sees and grasping an infinite number of details at a glance than his unobserving friend. He has reached this facility by exercise of his brain. He deliberately chose to enlarge his brain power in the line of observation, so he deliberately exercised that special faculty over and over with increasing attention and concentration. Now we have the result: a man learned in the lore of observation far above his fellow. Or, on the other hand, one can by stolid inaction, allow the delicate brain matter to harden and ossify until his whole life is barren and fruitless.

Every thought tends to become a material thing. Our desires are seed thoughts that have a tendency to sprout and grow and blossom and bear fruit. We are sowing these seeds every day. What shall the harvest be? Each of us today is the result of his past thinking. Later, we shall be the result of what we are now thinking. We create our own character, personality, and environment by the thought which we originate or entertain. Thought seeks its own. The law of mental attraction is an exact parallel to the law of atomic affinity. Mental currents are as real as electric, magnetic, or heat currents. We attract the currents with which we are in harmony.

Lines of least resistance are formed by the constant action of the mind. The activity of the brain reacts upon the particular faculty of the brain employed. The latent power of the mind is developed by constant exercise. Each form of its activity becomes more perfect by practice. Exercises for the development of the mind present a variety of motives for consideration. They involve the development of the perceptive faculties, the cultivation of the emotions, the quickening of the imagination, the symmetrical unfoldment of the intuitive faculty, which without being able to give a reason frequently impels or prohibits choice, and finally the power of mind may be cultivated by the development of the oral character.

"The greatest man," said Seneca, "is he who chooses right with invincible determination." The greatest power of mind, then, depends upon its exercise in moral channels, and therefore requires that every conscious mental effort should involve a moral end. A developed moral consciousness modifies consideration of motives and increases the force and continuity of action. Consequently, the well-developed symmetrical character necessitates good physical, mental, and moral health and this combination creates initiative, power, resistless force, and necessarily success.

It will be found that Nature is constantly seeking to express Harmony in all things, is forever trying to bring about an harmonious adjustment for every discord, every wound, every difficulty; therefore, when thought is harmonious, Nature begins to create the material conditions, the possession of which are necessary in order to make up an harmonious environment.

When we understand that mind is the great creative power, what does not become possible? With Desire as the great creative energy, can we not see why Desire should be cultivated, controlled, and directed in our lives and destinies? Men and women of string mentality who dominate those around them (and often those far removed from them) really emanate currents charged with power which, coming in contact with the minds of others, cause the desires of the latter to be in accord with the mind of the strong individuality. Great masters of men possess this power to a marked degree. Their influence is felt far and near and they secure compliance with their wishes by making others "want" to act in accord with them. In this way men of strong Desire and Imagination may and do exert powerful influence over the minds of others, leading the latter in the way desired.

No man is ever created without the inherent power in himself to help himself. The personality that understands its own intellectual and moral power of conquest will assert itself. It is this truth an enfamined world craves today. The possibility of asserting a slumbering intellectual courage that clearly discerns and a moral courage that grandly undertakes is open to all. There is a divine potency in every human being.

We speak of the sun as "rising" and "setting" though we know that this is simply an appearance of motion. To our senses, the earth is apparently standing still and yet we know it is revolving rapidly. We speak of a bell as a "sounding body," yet we know that all that the bell can do is to produce vibrations in the air. When these vibrations come at the rate of sixteen a second, they cause a sound to be heard in the mind. It is possible for the mind to hear vibrations up to the rate of 38,000 a second. When the number increases beyond this, all is silence again. So that we know that the sound is not in the bell. It is in our own mind.

We speak and even think of the sun as "giving light," yet we know it is simply giving forth energy that produces vibrations in the ether at the rate of four hundred trillion a second, causing what are termed "light waves," so that we know that what we call light is simply a mode of motion and the only light existent is the sensation caused in the mind by the motion of these waves. When the number of vibrations increases, the light changes in color, each change in color being caused by shorter and more rapid vibrations; so that although we speak of the rose as being red, the grass as being green, or the sky as being blue, we know that these colors exist only in our minds and are the sensations experienced by us as the result of the vibrations of light. When the vibrations are reduced below four hundred trillion a second, they no longer affect us as light, but we experience the sensation of heat.

So we have come to know that appearances exist for us only in our consciousness. Even time and space become annihilated, time being but the experience of succession, there being no past or future except as a thought relation to the present. In the last analysis, therefore, we know that one principle governs and controls all existence. Every atom is forever conserved; whatever is parted with must inevitably be received somewhere. It cannot perish and it exists only for use. It can go only where it is attracted and therefore required. We can receive only what we give and we may give only to those who can receive; and it remains with us to determine our rate of growth and the degree of harmony that we shall express.

The laws under which we live are designed solely for our advantage. These laws are immutable and we cannot escape from their operation. All the great eternal forces act in solemn silence, but it is within our power to place ourselves in harmony with them and thus express a life of comparative peace and happiness.

Difficulties, inharmonies, and obstacles indicate that we are either refusing to give out what we no longer need or refusing to accept what we require. Growth is attained through an exchange of the old for the new, of the good for the better; it is a conditional or reciprocal action, for each of us is a complete thought entity and the completeness makes it possible for us to receive only as we give. We cannot obtain what we lack if we tenaciously cling to what we have.

The Principle of Attraction operates to bring to us only what may be to our advantage. We are able to consciously control our conditions as we come to sense the purpose of what we attract and are able to extract from each experience only what we require for our further growth. Our ability to do this determines the degree of harmony or happiness we attain.

The ability to appropriate what we require for our growth continually increases as we reach higher planes and broader visions and the greater our ability to know what we require, the more certain we shall be to discern its presence, to attract it, and to absorb it. Nothing may reach us except what is necessary for our growth. All conditions and experiences that come to us do so for our benefit. Difficulties and obstacles will continue to come until we absorb their wisdom and gather from them the essentials of further growth. That we reap what we sow is mathematically exact. We gain permanent strength exactly to the extent of the effort required to overcome our difficulties.

The inexorable requirements of growth demand that we exert the greatest degree of attraction for what is perfectly in accord with us. Our highest happiness will be best attained through our understanding of and conscious cooperation with natural laws.

Our mind forces are often bound by the paralyzing suggestions that come to us from the crude thinking of the race and which are accepted and acted upon without question. Impressions of fear, of worry, of disability, and of inferiority are given us daily. These are sufficient reasons in themselves why men achieve so little—why the lives of multitudes are so barren of results, while all the time there are possibilities within them which need only the liberating touch of appreciation and wholesome ambition to expand into real greatness.

Women, perhaps even more than men, have been subject to these conditions. This is true because of their finer susceptibilities, making them more open to thought vibrations from other minds, and because the flood of negative and repressive thoughts has been aimed more especially at them.

But it is being overcome. Florence Nightingale overcame it when she rose in the Crimea to heights of tender sympathy and executive ability previously unknown among women. Clara Barton, the head of the Red Cross, overcame it when she wrought a similar work in the armies of the Union. Jenny Lind[1] overcame it when she showed her ability to command enormous financial rewards while at the same time gratifying the passionate desire of her nature and reaching the front rank of her day in musical art. And there is a long list of women singers, philanthropists, writers, and actresses who have proved themselves capable of reaching the greatest literary, dramatic, artistic, and sociological achievement.

Women as well as men are beginning to do their own thinking. They have awakened to some conception of their possibilities. They demand that if life holds any secrets, these shall be disclosed. At no previous time has the influence and potency of thought received such careful and discriminating investigation. While a few seers have grasped the great fact that mind is the universal substance—the basis of all things—never before has this vital truth penetrated the more general consciousness. Many minds are now

1 Jenny Lind (1820-1887) was known as "the world's sweetest singer." When she visited America in 1850, tickets for her show commanded fabulous prices. Toward the end of her life, she became a philanthropist.

striving to give this wonderful truth definite utterance. Modern science has taught us that light and sound are simply different intensities of motion and this has led to discoveries of forces within man that could not have been conceived of until this revelation was made.

A new century has dawned and now standing in its light man sees something of the vastness of the meaning of life—something of its grandeur. Within that life is the germ of infinite potencies. One feels convinced that man's possibility of attainment cannot be measured, that boundary lines to his onward march are unthinkable. Standing on this height, he finds that he can draw new power to himself from the Infinite energy of which he is a part.

Some men seem to attract success, power, wealth, and attainment with very little conscious effort; others conquer with great difficulty; still others fail altogether to reach their ambitions, desires, and ideals. Why is this so? Why should some men realize their ambitions easily, others with difficulty, and still others not at all? The cause cannot be physical, else the most perfect men physically would be the most successful. The difference, therefore, must be mental—must be in the mind. Hence, mind must be the creative force and must constitute the sole difference between men. It is mind, therefore, which overcomes environment and every other obstacle in the path of man.

When the creative power of thought is fully understood, its effect will seem to be marvelous. But such results cannot be secured without proper application, diligence, and concentration. The laws governing in the mental and spiritual world are as fixed and infallible as in the material world. To secure the desired results, then, it is necessary to know the law and to comply with it. A proper compliance with the law will be found to produce the desired result with invariable exactitude.

Scientists tell us that we live in the universal ether. This is formless of itself, but it is pliable and forms about us, in us, and around us according to our thought and word. We set it into activity by that which we think. Then that which manifests to us objectively is that which we have thought or said.

Thought is governed by law. The reason we have not manifested more faith is because of lack of understanding. We have not understood that everything works in exact accordance with definite law. The law of thought is as definite as the law of mathematics, or the law of electricity, or the law of gravitation. When we begin to understand that happiness, health, success, prosperity, and every other condition or environment are results, and that these results are created by thinking, either consciously or unconsciously, we shall realize the importance of a working knowledge of the laws governing thought.

Those coming into a conscious realization of the power of thought find themselves in possession of the best that life can give. Substantial things of a higher order become theirs and these sublime realities are so constituted that they can be made tangible parts of daily personal life. They realize a world of higher power and keep that power constantly working. This power is inexhaustible and limitless and they are therefore carried forward form victory to victory. Obstacles that seem insurmountable are overcome: Enemies are changed to friends, conditions are overcome, elements transformed, and fate is conquered.

The supply is inexhaustible and the demand can be made along whatever lines we may desire. This is the mental law of demand and supply.

Our circumstances and environment are formed by our thoughts. We have, perhaps, been creating these conditions unconsciously. If they are unsatisfactory, the remedy is to consciously alter our mental attitude and see our circumstances adjust themselves to the new mental condition. There is nothing strange or supernatural about this. It is simply the Law of Being. The thoughts that take root in the mind will certainly produce fruit after their kind. The greatest schemer cannot "gather grapes of thorns or figs of thistles." To improve our conditions we must first improve ourselves. Our thoughts and desires will be the first to show improvement.

To be in ignorance of the laws of vibration is to be like a child playing with fire or a man manipulating powerful chemicals without a knowledge of their nature and relations. This is universally true because Mind is the one great cause that produces all conditions in the lives of men and women.

Of course, mind creates negative conditions just as readily as favorable conditions, and when we consciously or unconsciously visualize every kind of lack, limitation, and discord, we create these conditions. This is what many are unconsciously doing all the time.

This law as well as every other law is no respecter of persons, but is in constant operation and is relentlessly bringing to each individual exactly what he has created. In other words, "Whatever a man soweth, that shall he also reap."

Arthur Brisbane[1] says, "Thought and its work include all the achievements of man."

Compare spirit and thought to the genius of the musician and the sound that issues from the musical instrument.

What the instrument is to the musician, the brain of the man is to the spirit that inspires thought.

However great the musician, the genius must depend for its expression upon the instrument that gives it reality in the physical world through sound waves produced in the material atmosphere, striking nerves that carry music to the brain.

Give Paderewski[2] a piano out of tune and he can give you only discord and lack of harmony. Or give to Paganini, the greatest violinist that ever lived, a violin out of tune and in spite of the genius of the musician you will hear only hideous, disagreeable sounds. The spirit of music must have the right instruments for its expression.

The spirit that inspires thought, the spirit of man, must have the right brain for its expression.

The more complicated and highly developed the instrument, the more displeasing is the result when the instrument is out of tune.

---

1 Arthur Brisbane (1864-1936) was a newspaper editor and writer known for his big, blaring headlines and atrocity stories.

2 Ignacy Jan Paderewski (1860-1941) was one of Poland's world renowned pianists and composers and was widely praised for his renditions of Chopin.

Among human beings, a highly developed brain out of tune is infinitely more painful and shocking than in the case of a human being with a mind in comparison feeble and simple.

Our minds are so little accustomed to deal with the abstract, we live so much in the material world, inanimate objects have so much meaning for us, that many human beings live and die without ever thinking at all of the spirit. Yet the spirit is the only real thing in the universe.

And thought is the expression of spirit, working through a more or less imperfect human being.

Bring yourself to think for some time earnestly of the nature and mysterious power of spirit. There is no thought more inspiring, fascinating, bewildering.

Consider the Falls of Niagra with their tremendous power, the vast moving machinery, the cities that are lighted, the blazing streets, the moving cars—all due apparently to the power in Niagra. Yet not due to that power in reality so much as to the spirit expressed in the thought of man. It was the spirit that harnessed Niagra. It was spirit that transferred the power of the Falls to distant cities.

Yet that spirit has neither shape nor weight, size nor color, taste nor smell. You ask a man, "What is the spirit?" and he must answer that it is nothing, since it occupies no space and cannot be seen or felt. And yet he must answer also that the spirit is everything. The world only exists as it is because we see it in the eyes of the spirit. The optic nerve takes a picture, sends it to the brain, and the spirit sees the picture.

It was spirit acting on the brain of Columbus and through him upon others that brought the first ship to America.

It is the spirit working and expressing itself through the thought of brains more and more highly developed that has gradually brought man from his former condition of savagery to his present comparative degree of civilization. And that same spirit, working in future ages through brains infinitely more superior to any that we can now conceive, will establish real harmony on this planet.

Yet you know that spirit exists and that it is you and that except for that spirit that animates you, picks you up when you fall, inspires you in success, and comforts you in failure and misfortune, there would be nothing at all in this life and you would not be different from one of the stones in the field or some of the dummies that the tailor sets in front of his store.

Compare the spirit and the material world as you see it with the genius that dwells in the brain of the great painter and the works that the painter has to do.

Every statue, painting, and church that Michelangelo created already existed in his spirit. But the spirit could not be content with that existence. It had to visualize itself; it had to see itself created.

The spirit really lives completely only when it sees itself reflected in the material world. All the mother love is in the spirit of woman. But it has complete existence only when the mother holds the child in her arms and see in reality—in flesh and blood—the being that she loves and has created.

The achievements of the greatest men are all locked up within them from the first, but the spirit of such men can reach full realization only when the spirit, acting through the brain and expressing itself through thought, created the work.

We know that all useful work is the result of sound thought. If we realize that thought itself is the expression of the spirit, we are moved by a sense of duty to give to that spirit the best possible expression of which we are capable, the best chance that it can have, dwelling in imperfect bodies and speaking through imperfect minds such as those we possess.

It is an inspiration to realize that men here on earth, gradually improving and becoming less animal and more spiritual as the centuries pass, are destined to develop in their own physical bodies instruments capable of interpreting properly the spirit that animates us.

Human beings improve from generation to generation. That we know. The improvement is due to the affection of fathers and mothers for each other and for their children.

This race of ours one hundred thousand years ago was made up of animal-like creatures with huge, projecting jaws, enormous teeth, small foreheads, and hideously shaped bodies. Gradually, through the centuries, we have changed. The brute has gradually disappeared and the prognathous face of man has become fatter. The jaw has gone in, the forehead has come out, and behind the forehead, gradually—thanks to the devotion and patient labor of women—we are developing a brain that will ultimately give decent and adequate expression to spirit.

Spirit and thought are identical in the sense that the genius of the musician and the sound that you hear when his music is played are identical. In music, the sound represents and interprets the musician's spirit. And the interpretation and the accuracy of that interpretation depend upon the orchestra, the violin, or the piano. When the instruments are out of tune, it is not the genius of the musician but a misinterpretation that you hear.

And with our human brains, most of them out of tune, most of them incapable of expressing anything but the merest, faintest reflection of true spiritual life, there is as yet very little harmony.

Through the perfected brain of man, the cosmic spirit, in which each of us is a conscious atom, will speak clearly and then this earth, our little corner of the universe, will be truly harmonious, governed by the spirit distinctly expressed and instantly obeyed.

This cosmic spirit can—and frequently does—operate through the brain of another. Many a man seems to be doing something very wonderful when in reality another man—another mind, not visible in the work, but actually at the work—does the heavy pulling.

You may see the salesman, the editor, the floor walker, the engineer, the architect—any kind of man engaged in any kind of work—apparently doing something wonderful.

Yet he is not doing it all. An unseen power—another man, another brain, perhaps some little man with a small body and a big head who keeps out of sight—is doing the work.

Every one of us without exception is pulled along or pushed ahead by some force unseen. It may be the man in the inside office, usually invisible. It may be the woman at home setting a good example, giving to the man at work the inspiration and the power that no one else can give. It may be the paternal affection, enabling a man to do for a child what he could not possibly do for himself.

Very often the power is one that has long disappeared from the earth, a father or mother whose energy and inspiration persists and does in the life of the son at work what the man could never have accomplished of his own accord.

> Cause and effect is as absolute and undeviating in the hidden realm of thought as in the world of visible and material things. Mind is the master weaver, both of the inner garment of character and the outer garment of circumstance.
>
> **—James Allen**

PART NINE

CAUSATION

Universal intelligence leaves its source to become embodied in material forms through which it returns to its source. Mineral life animated by electromagnetism is the first step of intelligence upward, toward its universal source. Universal energy is intelligent and this involuntary process by which matter is built-up is an intelligent process of nature that has for its specific purpose the individualization of her intelligence.

Stockwell[1] says:

"The basis of life and consciousness lies back of the atoms and may be found in the universal ether."

Hemstreet[2] says:

"Mind in the ether is no more unnatural than mind in flesh and blood."

Stockwell says:

"The ether is coming to be apprehended as an immaterial superphysical substance, filling all space, carrying in its infinite, throbbing bosom the specks of aggregated dynamic force called worlds. It embodies the ultimate spiritual principle and represents the unity of those forces and energies from which spring as their source all phenomena—physical, mental, and spiritual—as they are known to man."

Dolbear[3] in his great work on the ether says:

"Besides the function of energy and motion, the ether has other inherent properties out of which can emerge, under proper circumstances, other phenomena, such as life or mind or whatever may be in the substratum."

The microscopic cell, a minute speck of matter that is to be-

---

1 John Stockwell was an astronomer who became an instructor at the Case School of Applied Science, which was opened in 1880.
2 Charles Hemstreet was a scientists whose writings appeared extensively at the turn of the century.
3 Amos Dolbear contributed many notable inventions to the scientific world, including the static telephone, the electric gyroscope used to demonstrate the Earth's rotation, the opeidoscope, and a new system of incandescent lighting.

come man, has in it the promise and germ of mind. May we not draw the inference that the elements of mind are present in those chemical elements—carbon, oxygen, hydrogen, nitrogen, sulphur, phosphorus, sodium, potassium, chlorine—that are found in the cell? Not only must we do so, but we must go further, since we know that each of these elements and every other is built-up of one invariable unit, the electron, and we must therefore assert that mind is potential in the unit of matter—the electron itself.

Atoms of mineral matter are attracted to each other to form aggregates or masses. This attraction is called "chemical affinity." Chemical combinations of atoms are due to their magnetic relations to each other. Positive atoms will always attract negative atoms. The combination will last only so long as a still more positive force is not brought to bear on it to break it apart.

Two or more atoms brought into combination form a molecule, which is defined as "the smallest particle of a substance that can maintain its own identity." Thus, a molecule of water is a combination of two atoms of hydrogen and one atom of oxygen (H_2O).

In building a plant, nature works with colloid cells rather than with atoms, for she has built-up the cell as an entity just as she built the atom and the molecule as entities with which to work in mineral substance. The vegetable cell (colloid) has power to draw to itself from earth, air, and water whatever energies it needs for its growth. It therefore draws from mineral life and dominates it.

When vegetable matter is sufficiently refined to be receptive to still more of the universal intelligent energy, animal life appears. The plant cells have now become so plastic that they have additional capacities—those of individual consciousness and also additional powers, those of sensational magnetism. It draws its life forces from both mineral and plant life and therefore dominates them.

The body is an aggregate of cells animated by the spiritual magnetic life that tends toward organizing these cells into communities, and these communities into coordinated bodies that will operate the entire mass of the body as a conscious entity able to carry itself from one place to the other.

Atoms and molecules and their energies are now subordinated to the welfare of the cell. Each cell is a living, conscious entity capable of selecting its own food, of resisting aggression, and of reproducing itself.

As each cell has its individual consciousness, intuition, and volition, so each federated group of cells has a collective individual consciousness, intuition, and volition. Likewise, each coordinated group of federations, until the entire body has one central brain where the great coordination of all the "brains" takes place.

The body of an average human being is composed of some twenty-six trillions (26,000,000,000,000) of cells; the brain and the spinal cord by themselves consist of some two billion cells.

The biogenic law proves that every vertebrate, like every other animal, evolves from a single cell. Even the human organism, according to Haeckel, is at first a simple nucleated globule of plasm about 1.125 inches in diameter, barely visible to the naked eye as a tiny point. The ovum transmits to the child by heredity the personal traits of the mother, the sperm-cell those of the father; and this hereditary transmission extends to the finest characteristics of the soul as well as the body. What is plasm? What is this mysterious living substance that we find everywhere as the material foundation of the wonders of life? Plasm or protoplasm is, as Huxley rightly said, the physical basis of organic life. To speak more precisely, it is a chemical compound of carbon that alone accomplishes the various processes of life. In its simplest form, the living cell is merely a soft globule of plasm containing a former nucleus. As soon as it is fertilized, it multiplies by division and forms a community or colony of many special cells.

These differentiate themselves, and by their specialization or modification, the tissues that compose the various organs are developed. The developed, many-celled organisms of man and all higher animals resemble a social, civil community, the numerous single individuals of which are developed in various ways, but were originally only simple cells of one common structure.

All life on this earth, as Dr. Butler points out in *How the Mind Cures*, began in the form of a cell that consisted of a body animated by a mind. In the beginning and long afterward, the animating mind was the one we now call the subconscious. But as the forms grew in complexity and produced organs of sense, the mind threw out an addition, forming another part, the one we now call the conscious. While at first all living creatures had but one guide that they must follow in all things, this later addition to mind gave the creature a choice. This was the formation of what has been termed "free will."

Each cell is endowed with an individual intelligence that helps it carry on, as by a miracle, its complex labours. The cell is the basis of man, and this fact must be constantly borne in mind in dealing with the wonders of mental chemistry.

As a nation is made up of a large number of living individuals, so the body is made up of a large number of living cells. The citizens of a country are engaged in varied pursuits—some in the work of production, in field, forest, mine, factory; some in the work of distribution, in transportation, in warehouse, store, or bank; some in the work of regulation, in legislative halls, on the bench, in the executive chair; some in the work of protection, soldiers, sailors, doctors, teachers, preachers. Likewise, in the body, some cells are working on production: mouth, stomach, intestines, lungs, supplying food, water, air; some are engaged in distribution of supplies and elimination of wastes: heart, blood, lymph, lungs, liver, kidneys, skin; some perform the office of regulation: brain, spinal cord, nerves; some are occupied in protection: white blood corpuscles, skin, bone, muscle; there are also cells that are entrusted the reproduction of species.

As the vigour and welfare of a nation depend fundamentally on the vitality and efficiency and cooperation of its citizens, so the health and life of the body depend upon the vitality, efficiency, and cooperation of its myriad cells.

We have seen that the cells are gathered into systems and groups for the performance of particular functions essential to physical life and expression, such as we see in organs and tissues.

So long as the several parts all act together in concord and with due regard to one another and the general purposes of the organism, there is health and efficiency. But when from any cause discord arises, illness supervenes. Disease is lack of comfort and harmony.

In the brain and nervous system the cells are grouped in their action according to the particular functions that they are called upon to perform. It is in this way that we are able to see, to taste, to smell, to feel, and to hear. It is also in this way we are able to recall past experiences, to remember facts and figures, an so on.

In mental and physical health, these various groups of neurons work in fine harmony, but in *dis*-ease they do not. In normal conditions, the ego holds all these individual cells and groups, as well as systems of cells, in harmonious and coordinate action.

Disease represents dissociated organic action; certain system or groups, each of which is made up of a vast number of microscopic cells, begin functioning independently, and hence inharmoniously; and thus upset the tone of the whole organism. A single organ or system can thus get out of tune with the rest of the body and do serious harm. This is one kind of disease.

In a federation of any sort, efficiency and concord of action depend upon the strength and confidence accorded the central administration of its affairs; and just in proportion to the degree of failure to maintain these conditions are discord and confusion sure to ensue.

Nels Quevli makes this clear in *Cell Intelligence*. He says, "The intelligence of man is the intelligence possessed by the cells in his brain." If man is intelligent and by virtue thereof is able to combine and arrange matter and force so as to effect structures, such as houses and railroads, why is not the cell also intelligent when he is able to direct the forces of nature so as to effect the structures we see such as plants and animals? The cell is not compelled to act by reason of any chemical and mechanical force any more than is man. He acts by reason of will and judgment of his own. He is a separate living animal. Bergson in his "Creative Evolution" seems to see in matter and life a creative energy. If we stood at a distance watching a skyscraper gradually grow into completeness, we would say there must be some creative energy back of it, pushing the construction and, if we could never get near enough to see the men and builders at work, we would have no other idea of how that skyscraper came into existence except that it was caused by some creative energy.

The cell is an animal, very highly organized and specialized. Take the single cell called "amoeba" for instance. He has no machinery with which he can manufacture starch. He does, however, carry with him building material with which he can in an emergency save his life by covering himself with a coat of armor. Other cells carry with them a structure that is called chromatophore. With this instrument, these cells are able to manufacture starch from the crude substances of earth, air, and water by the aid of sunlight. From these facts, it must appear evident to the reader that the cell is a very highly organized and specialized individual and that to look at him from the point of view of being mere matter and force is the same as to compare the actions of a stone rolling down a hill with that of an automobile moving over a smooth pavement. One is compelled to move by reason of the force of gravitation, while the other moves by virtue of the intellect that guides it. The structures of life, like plants and animals, are built from the materials taken from the earth, air, and water, just as are the structures man builds, like railroads and skyscrapers. If we were asked how it is possible for man to effect the construction of these railroads and buildings, we would say that it is by reason of the fact that he is an intelligent being.

If the cell has gone through the same process of social organization and evolution as man, why is it not also the same intelligent being as man? Did you ever stop to think what takes place when the surface of the body is cut or bruised? The white blood cells—or corpuscles as they are called—who are the general caretakers of the body, whose duty it is to look after everything in general, such as the fighting of bacteria and disease germs and the general repair work, will sacrifice their own lives by thousands if necessary to save the body. They live in the body, enjoying complete liberty. They do not float in the bloodstream except when in a hurry to get somewhere, but move around everywhere as separate independent beings to see that everything goes right. If a bruise or cut happens, they are at once informed and rush to the spot by thousands and direct the repair work and if necessary they change their own occupation and take a different job, that of making connective tissue in order to bind the tissues together. In nearly every open sore, bruise, or cut, they are killed in great numbers in their faithful effort to repair and close up the wound. A text book on physiology briefly speaks of it as follows:

"When the skin is injured, the white blood cells form new tissue upon the surface, while the epithelium spreads over it from the edges, stopping growth and completing the healing process."

There seems to be no particular center in the body around which intelligence revolves. Every cell seems to be a center of intelligence and knows what its duties are wherever it is placed and wherever we find it. Every citizen of the cell republic is an intelligent, independent existence, and all are working together for the welfare of all. Nowhere can we find more absolute sacrifice of the lives of the individuals to the general welfare of all than we do in the cell republic. The results cannot be obtained in any other way nor at any less cost of individual sacrifice, so it is necessary to their social existence. The principle of individual sacrifice to common welfare has been accepted and agreed upon as the right thing and as their common duty, impartially distributed among them, and they perform their alloted work and duties regardless of their own individual comfort.

Mr. Edison says:

"I believe that our bodies are made up of myriad units of life. Our body is not itself the unit of life or a unit of life. Let me give you as an example the S.S. Mauretania.

"The Mauretania is not herself a living thing—it is the men in her that are alive. If she is wrecked on the coast, for instance, the men get out, and when the men get out it simply means that the 'life units' leave the ship. And so in the same way a man is not 'dead' because his body is buried and the vital principle, that is, the 'life units,' have left the body.

"Everything that pertains to life is still living and cannot be destroyed. Everything that pertains to life is still subject to the laws of animal life. We have myriads of cells and it is the inhabitants in these cells (inhabitants which themselves are beyond the limits of the microscope) that vitalize our body.

"To put it in another way, I believe that these life units of which

I have spoken band themselves together in countless millions and billions in order to make a man. We have too facilely assumed that each one of us is himself a unit. This, I am convinced, is wrong, even by the high-powered microscope, and so we have assumed that the unit is the man, which we can see, and have ignored the existence of the real life units, which are those we cannot see.

"No man today can set the line as to where 'life' begins and ends. Even in the formation of crystals, we see a definitely ordered plan of work. Certain solutions will always form a particular kind of crystal without variation. It is not impossible that these life entities are at work in the mineral and plant as in what we call the 'animal' world."

The idea is prevalent that both light and heat come all the way from the sun, a distance of 93,000,000 miles. If this were true, all space would be flooded with light, and no star would ever be visible, for stars are not visible in the light.

The sun is a great dynamo 886,000 miles in diameter. It turns on its axis like the planets, it sends electromagnetic currents throughout all solar space, which is something like six billion miles from end to end, and it is but one of thousands of similar systems of suns and planets, many of them much greater and all of them moving forward in space and all moving around one common center.

It is clear, then, that instead of giving light and heat the sun gives forth electrical energy only. This energy contacts with the atmosphere of the earth in the form of rays. As the earth is revolving at the incredible speed of more than a thousand miles an hour at its circumference, the atmosphere coming in contact with the electric rays of the sun causes friction, which produces both light and heat.

As the earth revolves at a constantly decreasing speed as we reach the poles, the friction becomes less and less, and so we find less light and less heat as the poles are reached, until at the poles there is little light or heat. What we know as light appears only in the atmosphere and not outside of it, and only in that part of the atmosphere that is turned toward the sun.

We know that as we ascend from the earth, the atmosphere becomes more rare and there is consequently less friction and therefore less light and less heat.

As the direct rays of electric energy from the sun reach only that part of the earth that is turned toward the sun, light appears only on that side. The other side of the earth being turned away from the sun, there is no friction and consequently no light, but as the earth turns upon its axis at the tremendous velocity of something like one thousand miles an hour, the atmosphere gradually comes in contact with the electrical rays from the sun and light gradually appears. The more perpendicular the rays strike the earth, the stronger the friction, the brighter the light, and the greater the heat. This solar phenomena we call morning, noon, and night.

This solar fluid is the ethereal atmosphere, or the ether, and is limited to the solar system; it is the medium for the transmission of the potencies originating in the various planets and holds in solution the basic elements of all life and thought.

This ether is the only possible fluid that is sufficiently subtle to carry the delicate vibrations that are constantly being broadcasted over the radio and which penetrate iron, wood, steel, and every other barrier, and which are not limited by wither space and time.

Each planet is also an electro-vital-dynamo, but the nature of the vibrations that they send depends upon the particular nature of that planet, as well as its ever changing position in the zodiac. These emanations are constantly being impressed upon all the worlds of our system by the perfect conductivity of the solar ether.

The sun is not only the source of electrical energy by which light and heat are developed, but it is the source of life itself. No life of any kind could exist on this planet without the energizing and vitalizing magnetism derived from the sun. As the earth approaches the sun in Spring, we see the result in the myriad plants and flowers and the verdure with which the fields are covered. The life-giving force becomes everywhere apparent.

The effect of this influence is seen in the temperament of the people inhabiting the globe. When the perpendicular rays reach the people, we find a cheerful, optimistic, "sunny" disposition; but as we reach the far north, where the absence of light and heat make life a struggle, we find the people correspondingly dark and gloomy.

Thus, we find that not only the sun, but Venus, Mars, Saturn, the Moon, and all of the other planets radiate their own peculiar characteristics. This influence in turn is reflected in the character of those who come under the influence of these vibrations.

As the nature of the energy that the sun radiates is in accordance with its intrinsic nature, so the nature of the vibrations sent out by the planets is in accordance with their intrinsic natures.

Venus has long been regarded as the Goddess of Love, consequently, the characteristics of those coming under her influence are affectionate, sympathetic, refined, and contented. Mars has long been known as the God of War, and his influence is therefore courageous, venturesome, aggressive, and fearless. The influence of the Moon is reflective, receptive, and productive; of Mercury, intellectual, accomplished, skillful, and clever; of Jupiter, generous, philanthropic, moral, charitable, and sincere; of Saturn, prudent, cautious, patient, and reserved; of Uranus, original, ingenious, talented, and intuitive; of Neptune, idealistic, mystical, inspirational, and peculiar.

As we all come under the influence of each of these planets to some extent, we all manifest many of these characteristics to some degree.

In addition to the influence of particular planets, there is the influence of the various combinations of planets. These are usually divided into Cardinal, Fixed, and Common signs.

The influence of the cardinal sign is to stir the latent forces into action, promote change, and create initiative.

The influence of the fixed sign is for stability. The individual may be slow and plodding, but he will be persistent; he will know no defeat; he will concentrate upon one point and pursue it to the end; his zeal will almost be fanatical.

The influence of the common sign is flexibility and change. This influence is purely mental or spiritual and gives purpose and incentive to action.

The cardinal type therefore is active, the common restless, and the fixed is rigid. As material success depends upon action, the important factors in the world's work are derived from this type. As stability is a necessary factor in important industrial undertakings, the fixed type frequently share the material and financial success with the cardinal type. The common type is, however, adverse to effort. They want adventure, change, and travel. They are therefore the promoters, who bring manufacturer and inventor together; they are the vendors and middlemen and agents who negotiate between buyer and seller.

They are also the sensitives and react more keenly to the experiences of life. They carry the heavier burden because they feel more. They participate in the issues of life to a greater degree because they carry not only their own burden, but the burdens of those around them. The greater possibilities of inner unfoldment, understanding, and development are always with the sensitive. The sensitive uses not only reason, but imagination, vision, intuition, and insight.

The fixed types are usually the materialists who are content with objective possessions and attainments. They use their reason and are interested in that only which can be measured or which can be seen, felt, handled. They are the doers rather than the dreamers and are utterly stable. They fill many responsible positions with great success and are valuable members of society.

Neither type is superior. They are simply different. Both are necessary.

Each planet has its own rate of vibration and its influence upon the earth depends upon the angle that it forms, certain angles causing the vibrations to be accelerated or diminished, magnified or retarded.

These angles of planetary influences have been found to produce effects just as certain and definite as the various angles in chemistry.

Thus, the seven planets give the seven rays or vibrations or tunes, and the earth is the organ upon which these notes are played, and the harmony or inharmony resulting therefrom is the influence which we call good or evil, as the effect is pleasing or the reverse.

It is the operation of these seemingly different influences that gave the Romans the idea of dualism of a Universe with two forces in it, one good, the other evil, and which they subsequently personalized and called God and Satan, resulting in much confusion of thought.

We now know, however, that there is but one Universal power and that the operation of this power is perfect. This power manifests in infinite diversity, form disappears and new form appears, but it is One Infinite Cosmic Substance and this substance is but the manifestation of one Cosmic Principle.

This, then, is the laboratory in which Nature is forever combining the spiritual forces that result in the infinite diversity on every side, for all are "parts of one stupendous whole."

There are those who seem to think that by force of Will they can coerce the law. That they can sow seed of one kind and by "Will Power" make it bear fruit of another, but the idea of forcing a compliance with out wishes by the power of the individual will is an inverted conception, which may appear to succeed for a while, but is eventually doomed to failure, because it antagonizes the very power which it is seeking to use.

PART TEN

EQUILIBRIUM

Thinking leads man to knowledge. He may see and hear, and read and learn whenever he pleases and as much as he pleases; he will never know anything of it except that which by thinking he has made the property of his own mind. Is it then saying too much if I say that man, by thinking only, becomes truly man? Take away thought from man's life and what remains?

—Pestalozzi

Nature is forever trying to bring about an equilibrium, and in accordance with this law we find constant action and reaction.

The concentration of matter implies the dissipation of motion; conversely, the absorption of motion implies the diffusion of matter.

This accounts for the entire cycle of changes passed through by every existence. Moreover, it applies to the entire cycle of each existence, as well as to each detail of its history. Both processes are going on at every instance; but always there is a differential result is favor of one or the other. And every change, even though it be only a transposition of parts, inevitably advances one of the factors.

The Law of Attraction eventually results in an equilibrium, the quantity of motion implied by dispersion must be as great as the quantity of motion implied by aggregation, or rather must be the same motion, taking now the molar form and now the molecular form; and from this result there arises the conception not only of local evolutions and dissolutions throughout our Sidereal System, but of general evolutions and dissolutions alternating indefinitely.

Giordano Bruno[1] was burned alive in Rome in 1600 for giving expression to the following thought:

"That which was seed at first becomes grass, the ear, then bread, nutritive juice, blood, animal, seed, embryo, man, corpse, then again earth, stone, or other mineral, and so forth. Herein we recognize therefore a thing which changes into all these things and essentially remains ever one and the same."

This eternal and ceaseless ebb and flow of minute particles, changeless in themselves, has been called the "food cycle." It is enough to remark of the changes and cycles through which matter passes in the Universe, and which man has partly followed by balance and measuring-rod, that they are without end and limit.

---

1 Giordano Bruno (1548-1600) was an Italian philosopher, astronomer, and occultist who was executed as a heretic because his ideas conflicted with church doctrine. During his trial, he said to the court, "Perhaps you, my judges, pronounce this sentence against me with greater fear than I receive it."

Dissolution and generation, destruction and reformation clasp hands everywhere in an endless circle. In the bread that we eat, in the air that we breathe, we draw in the matter that once built up the bodies of our forefathers. Nay, we ourselves give every day a portion of the matter forming our bodies to the outside world and shortly after we retake this substance or matter similarly given off by our neighbors.

Of the conquerers on the battlefield, we can literally say that they take advantage of their success by literally eating their enemies as daily bread, for the bones of the battlefields are often carted off in great quantities and converted into fertilizer.

All energy on this earth, organic or inorganic, is directly or indirectly derived from the sun. The flowing water, the driving wind, the passing clouds, the rolling thunder, and the flashing lightening, the falling rain, snow, dew, frost, or hail, the growth of plants, the warmth and motion of animal and human bodies, the combustion of wood, of coal, and everything else, is the result of solar energy.

Through the process of combustion, the total amount of the vanished sunshine laid up in wood or coal may again be evolved. The force that urges forward the locomotive is simply sunshine converted into power.

In 1857, Mr. Murray of London published a biography of the famous English engineer, George Stephenson, in which an interesting description of the light and heat cycle is given:

"On Sunday, just when the company had returned from church and were standing on the terrace overlooking the railway station, a train rushed by leaving a long line of white steam behind.

"'Now,' said Stephenson to Buckland, the well-known geologist, 'can you tell me what power moves that train?' 'Why,' replied the other, 'I suppose it is one of your big engines.' 'But what moves the engine?' 'Oh, probably one of your stout Newcastle engine-drivers.' 'What do you say to the light of the sun?' 'What do you mean?' 'Nothing else moves the engine,' said the great engineer, 'It is light which for thousands of years has accumulated in the earth—light which was inhaled by plants, that these during the time of their growth might fix the carbon, and which now, after having for thousands of years been buried in the coal beds of the earth, is again brought forth and set free to serve the great purposes of mankind, as here in the engine.'"

The same energy of the sun takes up the water from the ocean in the form of vapor. Water would ever remain in perfect equilibrium of it were not for the action of the sun. The rays of the sun falling upon the ocean convert the water into vapor, and this vapor is taken up into the atmosphere in the form of mist. The wind gathers it together in the form of clouds and takes it across the continent. Here, through changes of temperature, it is again converted into rain or snow.

Let anyone study the wonderful and beautiful forms of snowflakes or snowstars falling to the ground on a cold winter's day and he can convince himself that one day the forms are quite different from those of the day before or of the day after, although the conditions may differ but in the very slightest degree.

Nevertheless, this minute difference has sufficed to evolve these very different forms. It shows that, as Carus Sterne says, "Each of these fugitive forms is the exact expression of a special complex relation between the moisture, motion, pressure, temperature, rarity, electrical tension, and chemical composition of the air that prevailed during their formation.

"With a many-sidedness of ideas, which anyone engaged in the drawing of patterns and designs for fabrics might envy, the intrinsic faculties of the simplest and most indifferent compounds we know of show themselves thus in opposition to the moulding influences of the outer world."

The action of the sun again converts the snow into water and through the law of gravitation it descends from the mountains to the various rivers by which it eventually reaches the parent ocean from which it came.

These cycles are all governed by a law of periodicity. Everything has periods of birth, growth, fruitage, and decline. These periods are governed by the **Septimal Law**.

The Law of Sevens governs the days of the week, the phases of the moon, the harmonies of sound, light, heat, electricity, magnetism, and atomic structure. It governs the life of individuals and of nations, and it dominates the activities of the commercial world.

Statisticians know that every period of financial prosperity is followed by a period of depression, and they consequently have no difficulty in foretelling general conditions in the commercial world. We can apply the same law to our own lives and thereby come into an understanding of many experiences that would otherwise appear inexplicable.

Life is growth and growth is change. Each seven years period takes us into a new cycle. The first seven years is the period of infancy. The next seven the period of childhood, representing the beginning of individual responsibility. The next seven represents the period of adolescence. The fourth period marks the attainment of full growth. The fifth period is the constructive period, when men acquire property, possessions, a home and family. The next, from 35 to 42, is a period of reactions and changes, and this in turn is followed by a period of reconstruction, adjustment, and recuperation, so as to be ready for a new cycle of sevens, beginning with the fiftieth year.

There are many who think that the world is just about to pass out of the sixth period; that it will soon enter into the seventh period, the period of readjustment, reconstruction, and harmony; the period that is frequently referred to as the Millennium.

Numbers are symbols only. They indicate the quantity and quality of energy and their symbols apply to everything in the universe.

It takes seven periods to perfect the physical manifestation of any created thing, even an idea.

Madame Blavatsky[1], in her *Secret Doctrine*, and other occultists in other works, tell us that there are seven great cycles in the development of mankind upon the earth, each of which produce a Great Race; and each Great Race, in turn, is sub-divided into seven

---

1 Helena Petrovna Hahn (1831-1891) was the founder of Theosophy, which is a body of belief which holds that all religions are attempts by man to ascertain "the Divine", and as such each religion has a portion of the truth.

sub-races.

Among the various nations, these seven Creative Forces of the Cosmos have been identified with the Rulers of the seven sacred planets—the Sun, Moon, Mercury, Mars, Venus, Jupiter, and Saturn.

The Moon changes its appearance every seven days. It is a well known fact that the phases of the moon not only rule the tides and vegetation, but in the higher forms of life regulate the periodic functions of generations in general.

The number seven stands for the recognition of the oneness of the physical, mental, and spiritual being. It penetrates to the uttermost depths to reveal the mysteries of life. *Seven is the key number to Nature's Law of Cause and Effect.*

In many ways, there is an actual, tangible, demonstrable relationship between numbers, letters, and ideas; and all are acted upon and act upon the vibrations thus induced. These vibrations are both mental and physical.

Nature makes no mistakes. Her every manifestation presents some divine idea, and unwittingly our actions are made to conform to her laws. This eliminates the element of chance and all that we are and do is the result of the action of the definite unchanging laws and their reaction to our lives. All is in accordance with the One fundamental principle of life, which is motion, or vibration, and which is forever seeking equilibrium.

"The Universe," forcibly remarks the French philosopher Pascal, "is a circle whose center is everywhere and whose circumference is nowhere."

As matter is endless in time or eternal, so it is no less without beginning or end in space; in its real existence it withdraws from the limitations imposed on our finite mind by the conceptions of time and space, conceptions from which it cannot free itself in thought. Whether we inquire about or investigate the extension of matter in the minutest of the greatest, we nowhere find an end or a final form, whether we call to our aid experiment or reflection. When the discovery of the microscope or the juxtaposition of magnifying glasses opened up worlds unknown before and revealed to the gaze of the investigator a fineness and minuteness of organic life and organic form-elements undreamed of until then, man cherished the audacious hope of coming on the track of the final organic element, perhaps on the very basis of existence.

This hope disappeared in proportion to the improvement of our instruments. In the hundredth part of a drop of water was found a world of organic life, which, by their movements, left no doubt that they were not without the two chief marks of animal life, sensation, and will. The smallest of these under the highest magnifying power are barely recognizable as to their outlines; their internal organization remains wholly unknown to us. It is also unknown to us what yet smaller forms of living things can or may exist. "Shall we," asks Cotta, "with yet improved instruments see the Monads as giants in a dwarf-world of still smaller organisms?"

As the microscope guides us in the world of the minute, so does the telescope direct us in the world of the vast. Here also astronomers audaciously dreamed of penetrating to the very limits of the universe, but the more they perfected their instruments, the more immeasurably did the worlds expand before their astonished gaze. The light white mists seen by the naked eye in the vault of heaven were resolved by the telescope into myriads of stars, of worlds, of suns, of planetary systems; and the earth with its inhabitants, so fondly and proudly deemed the very crown and center of existence, fell from its fancied exaltation to a mere atom moving in immeasurable space. "All our experiments yield us not the slightest trace of a limit; each increased power of the telescope only opens to our gaze new realms of stars and nebulae, which, if not consisting of galaxies of stars, are self-illuminating matter."

PART ELEVEN

PHYSIOLOGY

Thought engenders thought. Place one idea upon paper, another will follow it, and still another, until you have written a page. You cannot fathom your mind. It is a well of thought which has no bottom. The more you draw from it, the more clear and fruitful it will be. If you neglect to think yourself, and use other people's thoughts, giving them utterance only, you will never know what you are capable of.

—G.A. Sala

One of the most interesting features of the human system is its series of manufacturing plants in which are produced the chemical agents necessary to mobilize the constituents of food. And it is a part of the fine natural economy that the secretions containing these chemical agents should serve several other purposes also. In general, each may be said to have an alternative effect upon the others, or at least upon the activities of the other plants; also, they act upon the inward-bound nerve paths as exciters of effects in both the conscious and the subconscious activities.

Radiant energy, whether consciously or subconsciously released from the body, becomes the medium of sensory impressions that flash back to the perceptive centers and there set up reactions that are interpreted by these centers according to their stage of development of self, and therefore they interpret these messages exactly as they are received, without attempt to "think" about them or to analyze them. The process is as mechanical as an impression made by the actinic rays of the sun on a photographic plate.

The general principle by which an idea is preserved is vibratory like all other phenomena of nature. Every thought causes vibrations that will continue to expand and contract in wave circles, like the waves started by a stone dropped in a pool of water. Waves form other thoughts may counteract it, or it may finally succumb of its own inanition.

Thought will instantly set in motion the finest of spiritual magnetism, and this motion will be communicated to the heavier and coarser densities and will eventually affect the physical matter of the body.

Life is not created—it simply is. All nature is animate with this force we call "life." The phenomena of life on this physical plane, with which we are chiefly concerned, are produced by the involution of "energy" into "matter," and matter is, itself, an involution of energy.

But when the stage of matter is reached in the process of Nature's involution, matter then begins to evolve forms under the action upon it and within it. So that growth and life are the results of a simultaneous integration of matter and energy. Evolution starts with the lowest form of matter and works upward through refining processes to serve as a matrix of energy.

The internal secretions constitute and determine much of the inherited powers of the individual and their development. They control physical and mental growth and all the metabolic processes of fundamental importance. They dominate all the vital functions of man. They cooperate in an inanimate relationship that may be compared to an interlocking directorate. A derangement of their functions, causing an insufficiency of them, an excess, or an abnormality upsets the entire equilibrium of the body, with transformed effect upon the mind and the organs. Blood chemistry of our time is a marvel undreamed of a generation ago.

These achievements are a perfect example of accomplished fact contradicting all former prediction and criticism. One of the greatest advances of modern medicine has been the study of the processes and secretions of the hitherto obscure ductless glands. Endocrinology, as this study is called, has thrown much valuable light upon certain abnormal physical conditions about which science had until now been in the dark. We now know that most of the freaks of nature we see on exhibition are such owing to endocrine disturbance—the disturbance of the ductless glands. The bearded lady, a victim of pogoniasis; the victims of obesity and of skeletonization; of acromegalis, or giantism; of micromegalia or liliputianism—all such evolutional deviations are due to subnormalities or abnormalities of the chemical elements that the glands produce and send into the blood-stream.

These are no mere theories, for they have been rigorously tested in the laboratories of science. As Sir William Osler[1], one of the world's most illustrious luminaries of knowledge, has said:

> For man's body, too, is a humming hive of working cells, each with its specific function, all under central control of the brain and heart, and all dependent on materials called hormones (secreted by small, even insignificant looking structures) which lubricate the wheels of life. For example, remove

---

1 Sir William Osler (1849-1919) was a superb diagnostician and clinician whose book, *The Principles and Practice of Medicine*, revolutionized the medical curriculum of the United States.

> the thyroid gland just below the Adam's apple, and you deprive man of the lubricants which enable his thought-engines to work. It is as if you cut off the oil supply of a motor, and gradually the stored acquisitions of his mind cease to be available, and within a year he sinks into dementia. The normal processes of the skin cease, the hair falls, the features bloat, and the paragon of animals is transformed into a shapeless caricature of humanity.

These essential lubricators, of which a number are now known, are called hormones—you will recognize from its derivation how appropriate is the term. The name is derived from the Greek verb meaning "to rouse or set in motion." The name was given by Starling and Bayliss, two great Englishmen noted for their research work in endocrinology. Cretins (dwarfed imbeciles) can be cured by the administration, internally, of the thyroid glands of sheep with truly miraculous results; because cretinism is caused by the lack or absence of thyroid gland secretions.

As an instance of the fascination of these studies, consider the conception that the thyroid played a fundamental part in the change of sea creatures into land animals. Feeding the Mexican axolotl, a purely aquatic newt, breathing through gills, on thyroid, quickly changes it into the ambystoma, a terrestrial salamander breathing by means of lungs.

The endocrine glands produce secretions that enter the bloodstream and vitally affect the bodily structure and functions. The pituitary is a small gland, located near the center of the head directly under the third ventricle of the brain, where it rests in a depression in the bony floor-plate of the skull. Its secretions have an important part in the mobilizing of carbohydrates, maintaining blood pressure, stimulating other glands, and maintaining the tonicity of the sympathetic nerve system. Its under, or over, activity during childhood will produce marked characteristics in the body structure and, what concerns us more, equally marked characteristics of mental development and function.

The thyroid gland is located at the frontal base of the neck, extending upward in a sort of semicircle on both sides, with the parathyroids near the tips. The thyroid secretion is important in mobilizing both proteids and carbohydrates; it stimulates other glands, helps resist infections, affects hair growth, and influences the organs of digestion and elimination. It is a strongly determining factor in the all-around physical development, and also in the mental functioning. A well-balanced thyroid goes a long way toward insuring an active, efficient, smoothly coordinated mind and body.

The adrenal glands are located just above the small of the back. These organs have been called by some writers the "decorative glands," since one of their functions appears to be that of keeping the pigments of the body in proper solution and distribution. But of greater importance is the agency of the adrenal secretion in other directions. It contains a most valuable blood pressure agent; it is a tonic to the sympathetic nerve system, hence to the involuntary muscles, heart, arteries, intestines, and so on; as well as to the perceptive paths. It responds to certain emotional excitement by an immediate increase in volume of secretion, thus increasing the energy of the whole system, and preparing it for effective response.

The cerebro-spinal nervous system is the telephone system of the conscious mind; it is a very complete wiring system for communication from the brain to every part of the body, especially the terminals. It is the intelligence department of self-conscious man.

The sympathetic nervous system is the system of the subconscious mind. Behind the stomach and in front of the spine is the center of the system known as the "Solar Plexus." It is composed of two masses of brain substance, each in the shape of a crescent. They surround an artery whose function it is to equalize the blood pressure of all the abdominal organs.

Just as the brain and the voluntary nervous system constitute the apparatus of self-conscious man, in like manner the solar plexus and the sympathetic system comprise the special apparatus of the subconscious mind.

The function of the sympathetic nervous system is to maintain the equilibrium of the body, to act as a balance wheel, to prevent over- or under-action of the cerebro-spinal system. As it is directly affected by emotional states such as fear, anger, jealousy, or hatred, these may easily throw out of gear the operation of the automatic functions of the body. That is to say that emotional states such as joy, fear, anger, and hatred may upset such functions of the body as digestion, blood circulation, general nutrition, and so forth.

"Nerves" and all the unpleasant experiences that follow in the way of bodily discomfort and ill health are caused by negative emotions, such as fear, anger, hatred, and the like; they break down the resistance that has been offered by the various plexii which, when in normal working order, have a definite capacity to inhibit the effect of such emotions.

The sympathetic system is the apparatus whose function it is to maintain the body in a normal and healthy working order and to replace the wastage due to ordinary wear and tear, both emotional and physical. The kind of emotions that we entertain is therefore of great importance: if positive, they are constructive; if negative, they are destructive.

Happiness, prosperity, and contentment are the result of clear thinking and right action, for the thought precedes and predetermines the nature of the action. A little artificial stimulation in the form of intoxicating liquor may temporarily still the senses and thus serve to confuse the issue, but as in economics and mechanics where every action is followed by a reaction, so in human relations and every action is followed by an equal reaction, and so we have come to know that the value of things depends upon the recognition of the value of persons. Whenever a creed becomes current that things are of more importance than people, programs become fixed that set the interest of wealth above the interests of people, this action must necessarily be followed by a reaction.

But because the opium traffic furnishes millions of revenue for Englishmen, millions of Chinese must be sacrificed, and because the sale and distribution of alcohol furnishes million dollar accounts for large banks and trust companies, $100,000.00 fees for corporation attorneys, because it makes it possible to lead large masses of men to the polls for the purpose of voting for political parties that are both morally and politically bankrupt, there are those who would again inflict this deadly curse upon the citizens of our country.

Dr. Woods Hutchinson tells us that the death rate for the United States has fallen in the last three years from 14.2 to 12.3 a thousand, which represents a saving of over 200,000 lives a year since the brewers' business was closed down. "Almost unanimous reports from public school teachers, school and district nurses, welfare workers among the poor, intelligent police chiefs, and heads of charitable organizations show that never, in all their experience, has there been so striking an improvement in the feeding, the clothing, the general comfort and welfare of school children as within the last two years."

And yet there are those who favor the modification of the Volstead Act. There is probably not a single individual in existence whose thinking processes are in such an infantile stage of development that he does not know that when a door has been partly opened it requires but the pressure of the little finger to push it wide open, so that modification is but another word for annulment with all of its physical, mental, moral, and spiritual degradation and disaster, and all of the sorrow, suffering, infamy, shame, and horror that this most monstrous curse has inflicted upon suffering humanity.

Experience has decided that any stimulus applied statedly to the stomach, which raises its molecular tones above the point at which it can be sustained by food and sleep, produces, when it has passed away, debility—a relaxation of the over-worked organ, proportioned to its preternatural excitement. The life-giving power of the stomach fails of course as much below the tone of cheerfulness and health, as it was injudiciously raised above it. If the experiment be repeated often, it produces an artificial tone of stomach, essential to cheerfulness and muscular vigor, entirely above the power of the regular sustenance of nature to sustain, and creates a vacuum which nothing can fill but the destructive power which made it; and when protracted use has made the difference great between the natural and the artificial tone, and habit has made it a second nature, the man is a drunkard and in ninety-nine instances in a hundred is irretrievably undone.

Beer has been recommended as a substitute and a means of leading back the captive to health and liberty. But though it may not create intemperate habits as soon, it has no power to allay them. It will even finish what alcohol has begun and with this difference only, that it does not rasp the vital organs with quite so keen a file and enables the victim to come down to his grave by a course somewhat more dilatory and with more of the good-natured stupidity of the idiot and less of the demoniac frenzy of the madman.

Wine has been prescribed as a means of decoying the intemperate from the ways of death. But habit cannot be thus cheated out of it dominion, nor ravening appetite be amused down to a sober and temperate demand. It is not true that wine will restore the intemperate or stay the progress of the disease. Enough must be taken to screw up nature to the tone of cheerfulness, or she will cry "Give!" with an importunity not to be resisted; and long before the work of death is done, wine will fail to minister a stimulus of sufficient activity to rouse the flagging spirits, or will become acid on the enfeebled stomach, and whiskey and brandy will be called in to hasten to its consummation the dilatory work of self-destruction.

In one of Tolstoi's essays, we find that the seeing, spiritual being, whose manifestation we commonly call conscience, always points with one end towards right and with the other towards wrong, and we do not notice it while we follow the course it shows: the course form wrong to right. But one need only do something contrary to the indication of conscience, to become aware of this spiritual being, which then shows how the animal activity has diverged from the direction indicated by conscience. And as a navigator, conscious that he is on the wrong track, cannot continue to work the oars, engine, or sails till he has adjusted his course to the indications of the compass, or has obliterated his consciousness of this divergence—each man who has felt the duality of his animal activity and his conscience can continue his activity only by adjusting that activity to the demands of conscience or by hiding from himself the indications conscience gives him of the wrongness of his animal life.

All human life, we may say, consists solely of these two activities: (1) bringing one's activities into harmony with conscience, or (2) hiding form one's self the indications of conscience in order to be able to continue to live as before.

Some do the first, others the second. To attain the first, there is but one means: moral enlightenment—the increase of light in one's self and attention to what it shows; for the second (to hide from one's self the indications of conscience), there are two means: one external and the other internal. The external means consists in occupations that divert one's attention from the indications given by conscience; the internal method consists in darkening conscience itself.

As a man has two ways of avoiding seeing an object that is before him (either by diverting his sight to other, more striking objects, or by obstructing the sight of his own eyes), just so a man can hide from himself the indications of conscience in two ways: either by the external method of diverting his attention to various occupations, cares, amusements, or games; or by the internal method of obstructing the organs of attention itself. For people of dull, limited moral feeling, the external diversions are often quite sufficient to enable them not to perceive the indications conscience gives of the wrongness of their lives. But for morally sensitive people, those means are often insufficient.

The external means do not quite divert attention from the consciousness of discord between one's life and the demands of conscience. This consciousness hampers one's life and people, in order to be able to go on living as before, have recourse to the reliable, internal method, which is that of darkening conscience itself by poisoning the brain with stupefying substances.

One is not living as conscience demands, yet lacks the strength to reshape one's life in accord with its demands. The diversions that might distract attention from the consciousness of this discord are insufficient or have become stale, and so (in order to be able to live on, disregarding the indications conscience gives of the wrongness of their life) people stop the activity of the organs through which conscience manifests itself, as a man by covering his eyes hides from himself what he does not wish to see.

Not in the taste, nor in any pleasure, recreation, or mirth they afford, lies the cause of the world-wide consumption of opium, wince, and tobacco, but simply in man's needs to hide from himself the demands of conscience.

Not only do people stupefy themselves to stifle their own consciences, but when they wish to make others commit actions contrary to conscience, they intentionally stupefy them—that is, arrange to stupefy people in order to deprive them of conscience.

When a fortified place has been captured, the soldiers do not sack it and slay the defenseless old men and children. Orders are often given to make them drunk and then they do what is expected of them.

Everyone knows people who have taken to drink in consequence of some wrongdoing that has tormented their conscience. Anyone can notice that those who lead immoral lives are more attracted than others by stupefying substances. Bands of robbers or thieves cannot live without intoxicants.

In a word, it is impossible to avoid understanding that the use of stupefiers, in large or small amounts, occasionally or regularly, in the higher or lower circles of society, is evoked by one and the same cause: the need to stifle the voice of conscience in order not to be aware of the discord existing between one's way of life and the demands of one's conscience.

In that alone lies the reason of the widespread use of all stupefying substances, and among the rest of tobacco, probably the most generally used and most harmful.

Any smoker may detect in himself the definite desire to stupefy himself with tobacco at certain, specially difficult moments. I look back at the days when I used to smoke; when was it that I felt a special need of tobacco? It was always at moments when I did not wish to remember certain things that presented themselves to my recollection, when I wished to forget—not to think. I sit by myself doing nothing and know I ought to set to work, but didn't feel inclined to, so I smoke and go on sitting. I have promised to be at someone's house by five o'clock, but I have stayed too long somewhere else; I have remembered that I have missed the appointment, but I do not like to remember it, so I smoke. I get vexed and say unpleasant things to someone and know I am doing wrong and see that I ought to stop, but I want to give vent to my irritability, so I continue to smoke and continue to be irritable. I play at cards and lose more than I intended to risk, so I smoke. I have placed myself in an awkward position, have acted badly, have made a mistake, and ought to acknowledge the mess I am in and thus escape from it, but I do not like to acknowledge it, so I accuse others—and smoke. I write something and am not quite satisfied with what I have written. I ought to abandon it, but I wish to finish what I have planned to do—so I smoke. I dispute and see that my opponent and I do not understand and cannot understand one another, but I wish to express my opinion, so I continue to talk—and I smoke.

Emancipation from this evil will be an epoch in the life of humanity—and that epoch seems to be at hand. The evil is recognized. An alteration has already taken place in our perception concerning the use of stupefying substances. People have understood the terrible harm of these things and are beginning to point them out, and this almost unnoticed alteration in perception will inevitably bring about the emancipation of men from the use of stupefying things and will enable them to open their eyes to the demands of their consciences and they will begin to order their lives in accord with their perceptions.

Physiology has scientifically demonstrated the connection between the brain and the mind in the well-known experiments of vivisection performed by physiologists on the brains of living animals, which experiments defy all contradiction. The most famous among these experiments are those of the French physiologist Flourens, who experiments on animals whose physical constitution enables them to endure considerable injuries to cranium and brain.

He cut away the upper portions of the brain, layer by layer, one after another, and it is not saying too much to assert that as the layers disappeared one by one, the mental faculties of the animals diminished at the same time and eventually disappeared altogether.

Thus Flourens[1] succeeded in reducing fowls to a condition in which every mental function and every capacity of receiving sensational impressions or of performing any conscious action were completely annihilated, and yet physical life went on. The animals remained motionless at any spot in which they were placed

1 Marie Jean Pierre Flourens (1794-1867) was a French physiologist and the founder of experimental brain science and a pioneer in anesthesia.

as though they were in a deep sleep; they responded to no external stimulus and were kept alive by artificial feeding; they led, as it were, a mere vegetable existence. Thus they remained alive for months and years and increased in weight and size of the body.

Similar experiments have been successfully performed on higher animals, that is to say, on mammals. "If the cerebral hemispheres of a mammal are cut away piecemeal," says Valentin, "the mental activity descends all the deeper, the further the quantitative loss extends. As a rule, when the ventricles are reached, complete unconsciousness supervenes." What stronger proof of the connection between mind and brain can there exist than that of the anatomist's scalpel?

Where Truth Abides

Truth is within ourselves; it takes no rise
From outward things, whate'er you may believe,
There is an inmost center in us all,
Where Truth abides in fullness; and around,
Wall upon wall, the gloss flesh hems it in,
This perfect clear conception—which is Truth.
A baffling and perverting carnal mesh
Blinds it, and makes all error; and, to know
Rather consists in opening out a way
Whence the imprisoned splendor may escape,
Than in effecting entry for a light
Supposed to be without.

—Robert Browning

PART TWELVE

The PSYCHOLOGY of MEDICINE

The PSYCHOLOGY of MEDICINE

To the development of radio communication is largely due the fillip to the imagination of science and the dawning of an idea that a few years ago would have been considered revolutionary and subversive of all the established traditions of medicine.

"The psychical method has always played an important, though largely unrecognized, part in therapeutics. It is from faith, which buoys up the spirits, sets the blood flowing more freely, and the nerves playing their parts without disturbance, that a large part of all cures arise. Despondency or lack of faith will often sink the stoutest constitution almost to death's door; faith will enable a bread pill or a spoonful of clear water to do almost miracles of healing, when the best medicines have been given over in despair. The basis of the entire profession of medicine is faith in the doctor and his drugs and his methods."[1]

Charles Richet[2], professor of physiology in the University of Paris, is blazing the trail for those hardy pioneering scientists who are now exploring the borderland of the senses. In a recent address before the International Congress of Physiologists in Edinburgh, as quoted by *The Lancet*, a leading British medical journal, Dr. Richet said:

"The thesis which I wish to sustain and to prove by the experimental method is that there may be a knowledge of reality obtained by other means than by the ordinary channels of the senses. Everyone know that the external world is accessible to us by our senses, by vision, hearing, and touch, and to a less extent by smell and taste. No other ways are known. It is the universal opinion that we can have no other notion of the reality that surrounds us except through our five senses, and that any fact must remain forever unknown unless sound, touch, or vision has reveled it to us. This is the classic and at the same time popular idea. It is formal

1 From *The Healing Wisdom of Dr. P.P. Quimby*. Dr. Phineas Parkhurst Quimby believed that false beliefs created disease. His therapy was to show his patients the errors in their beliefs.
2 Charles Robert Richet (1850-1935) was a French physiologist who won the 1913 Nobel Prize for Physiology or Medicine for his work on anaphylaxis, his term for the sometimes fatal reaction by a sensitized individual to a second injection of an antigen.

and exclusive, without itself ever having been demonstrated. To admit that a knowledge of occurrences can arrive at our consciousness by any other means than those of the senses is a daring and revolutionary proceeding, and yet this is the thesis that I am about to maintain.

"The access to our subconscious intelligence of mysterious vibrations is an unusual phenomenon, but it is a phenomenon which is not in contradiction to anything. It is a new truth, that is all. And this new truth is wonderfully in agreement with the amazing notions which modern physics opens to us. At this moment I cannot hear any concert in this hall, nor do you. You might even assert that there are no musical vibrations here. What a mistake! If a wireless receiver were placed here we should all immediately hear a concert that is taking place perhaps three miles, or even 100 miles away. The receiver proves that the vibrations are present. Thus it is with those mysterious paths of consciousness. They do not reach us, but they are there. Only a sensitive person, in other words, a receiver, is needed to prove their reality. Therefore, do not hesitate to accept this new fact that unknown vibrations strike an intelligence and bring to it unexpected knowledge.

"Can physiologists and medical men assert that they have completed the physiology of the brain; that there is nothing further to be discovered about it, and that they have delimited all the modes of vibration of which it is capable? The brain is a much more complicated machine than we are wont to consider it in our innocence. Why may not this marvelous machine be sometimes capable of receiving vibrations which pass unknown to consciousness?"

Our problem would be more simple, and the doctors, with their wide knowledge and splendid service, would have solved the problem long ago, had it been a purely physical one; but unfortunately it is a mental problem long before it becomes a physical one. As we continue to exercise our capacity for response we shall find it necessary to treat our thoughts and emotions if we are to establish health upon a firm basis.

For instance, it is commonly recognized that worry or continued negative emotional excitement will disorganize digestion. When the digestion is normal, the feeling of hunger will stop, will be inhibited when we have eaten as much as we need, nor will we fell hunger again until we actually require food. In such cases, our inhibiting center is working properly. But if we get dyspeptic, this inhibiting center has ceased to function, and we are hungry all the time with the consequent tendency to overwork and already impaired digestive apparatus. Mankind is continually experiencing such small disturbances. They are strictly local and attract small attention at the great center. They come and go—and properly so—without drawing from the organism as a whole much consideration. But if the disorder has grown out of a deep-rooted cause that cannot easily be removed, disease of a more serious nature will ensue. Under such circumstances, by reason of its seriousness and long continuance, the trouble involves all parts of the organism and may threaten its very life. When it reaches this point, if the administration at the grand center is vigorous and determined and wise, then the disturbance cannot long endure; but if there is weakness at that center, the whole federation may go down with a crash.

Dr. Lindlahr[1] says that "Nature Cure Philosophy presents a rational concept of evil, its cause and purpose, namely; that it is brought on by violation of Nature's laws, that it is corrective in its purpose that it can be overcome only by compliance with the Law. There is no suffering, disease, or evil of any kind anywhere unless the law has been transgressed somewhere by someone."

These transgressions of the law may be due to ignorance, to indifference, or to willfulness and viciousness. The effect will always be commensurate with the causes.

The science of natural living and healing shows clearly that what we call disease is primarily Nature's effort to eliminate morbid matter and to restore the normal functions of the body; that the processes of disease are just as orderly in their way as everything else in Nature; that we must not check or suppress them, but cooperate with them. Thus we can, slowly but laboriously, the all-important lesson that "obedience to the law" is the only means of

---

1 Henry Lindlahr (1862 - 1924) was a pioneer in natural medicine. He believed that the cure for many diseases was a return to nature of which a natural diet was most important.

prevention of disease, and the only cure.

The Fundamental Law of Cure, the Law of Action and Reaction, and the Law of Crisis, as revealed by the Nature Cure Philosophy, impress upon us the truth that there is nothing accidental or arbitrary in the process of health, disease, and cures; that every changing condition is either in harmony or in discord with the laws of our being; that only by complete surrender and obedience to the law can we master the law and attain and maintain perfect physical health.

In our study of the cause and character of disease we must endeavour to begin at the beginning—and that is life itself. For the process of health, disease, and cure are manifestations of that which we call life and vitality.

There are two prevalent, but widely differing conceptions of the nature of life or vital force: the material and the vital.

The former looks upon life or vital force with all its physical, mental, and psychical phenomena as manifestations of the electric, magnetic, and chemical activities of the physical-material electric elements composing the human organism. From this viewpoint, life is a sort of "spontaneous combustion", or, as one scientist expressed it, a "succession of fermentations."

This materialistic conception of life, however, has already become obsolete among the more advanced biologists as a result of the discoveries of modern science, which are fast bridging the chasm between the material and the spiritual realms of being.

The vital conception of Life or Vital Force on the other hand, regards it as the primary force of all forces, coming from the central source of all power.

This force, which permeates, warms, and animates the entire created universe, is the expression of the Divine Will, the Logos, the Word, of the Great Creative Intelligence. It is this Divine Energy that sets in motion the whirls in the ether, the electric corpuscles and ions that make up the different atoms and elements of matter.

These corpuscles and ions are positive and negative forms of electricity. Electricity is a form of energy. It is intelligent energy, otherwise it could not move with that unvarying, wonderful precision in the electrons of the atoms as in the suns and planets of the sidereal universe.

If this supreme intelligence should withdraw its energy—the electrical charges (forms of energy)—and with it the atoms and elements, the entire material universe would disappear in the flash of a moment.

From this it appears that crude matter, instead of being the source of life and of all its complicated mental and spiritual phenomena, is only an expression of the Life Force, itself a manifestation of the Great Creative Intelligence which some call God, others Nature, the Oversoul, Brahma, Prana, and other sundry names, each one according to his understanding.

It is this supreme power and intelligence acting in and through every atom, molecule, and cell in the human body, which is the true healer, this "*vis medicatrix naturae*" which always endeavors to repair, to heal, and to restore the perfect type. All that the physician can do is to remove obstructions and to establish normal conditions within and about the patient so that the power within can do its work to the best advantage.

In the final analysis, all things in Nature, from a fleeting thought or emotion to the hardest piece of diamond or platinum, are modes of motion or vibration. A few years ago, physical science assumed that an atom was the smallest imaginable part of a given element of matter; that although infinitesimally small, it still represented solid matter. Now, in the light of better evidence, we have good reason to believe that there is no such thing a solid matter; that every atom is made up of charges of negative and positive electricity acting in and upon an omnipresent ether; that the difference between an atom of iron and of hydrogen, or any other element, consists solely in the number of electrical charges or corpuscles it contains and on the velocity with which these vibrate around one another.

Thus the atom, which was thought to be the ultimate particle of solid matter, is found to be a little universe in itself in which corpuscles of electricity rotate or vibrate around one another like the suns and planets in the sidereal universe. This explains what we mean when we say life and matter are vibratory.

What we call "inanimate nature" is beautiful and orderly because it plays in tune with the score of the Symphony of Life. Man alone can play out of tune. This is his privilege or his curse, as he chooses, by virtue of his freedom of choice and action.

We can now better understand the definitions of health and of disease given in the Catechism of Nature Cure as follows:

"Health is normal and harmonious vibration of the elements and forces composing the human entity and the physical, mental, moral, and spiritual planes of being in conformity with the constructive principle of Nature applied to individual life.

"Disease is abnormal or inharmonious vibration of the elements and forces composing the human entity on one or more planes or being in conformity with the destructive principle of Nature applied to individual life."

The question naturally arising here is, *Normal or abnormal vibration with what?*

The answer is that the vibratory conditions of the organism must be in harmony with Nature's established harmonic relations in the physical, mental, moral, spiritual, and psychical realms of human life and action.

PART THIRTEEN

MENTAL CHEMISTRY

Though an inheritance of acres may be bequeathed, and inheritance of knowledge and wisdom cannot. The wealthy man may pay others for doing his work for him, but it is impossible to get his thinking done for him by another, or to purchase any kind of self-culture.

MENTAL CHEMISTRY

Chemistry is the science which treats of the intra-atomic or the intra-molecular changes that materials things undergo under various influences.

Mental is defined as "of or pertaining to the mind, including intellect, feeling, and will, or the entire rational nature."

Science is knowledge gained and verified by exact observation and correct thinking.

Mental chemistry is, therefore, the science which treats of the changes that conditions undergo through the operation of the mind.

As the transformations that are brought about in applied chemistry are the result of the orderly combination of materials, it follows that mental chemistry brings about results in a like manner.

Any conceivable number may be formed with the Arabic numerals 1, 2, 3, 4, 5, 6, 7, 8, 9, 0.

Any conceivable thought may be expressed with the 26 letters of the alphabet.

Any conceivable thing can be organized with the 14 elements and always and only by the proper grouping of electrons into molecules.

When two or more molecules are grouped, a new individuality is created, and this individuality that has been called into being possesses characteristics that are not possessed by either of the elements that gave it being.

Thus one atom of sodium and one of chlorine give us salt, and this combination alone can give us salt, and no other combination of elements can give us salt, and salt is something very different from either of the elements of which it is composed.

What is true in the inorganic world is likewise true in the organic—certain conscious processes will produce certain effects and the result will invariable be the same. The same thought will always be followed by the same consequence and no other thought will serve the purpose.

This must necessarily be true because the principle must exist independently of the organs through which they function. Light must exist—otherwise there could be no eye. Sound must exist—otherwise there could be no ear. Mind must exist—otherwise there could be no brain.

Mental action is therefore the interaction of the individual upon the Universal Mind, and as the Universal Mind is the intelligence which pervades all space and animates all living things, this mental action and reaction is the law of causation.

It is the Universal Chemist, but the principle of causation does not obtain in the individual mind but in the Universal Mind. It is not an objective faculty, but a subjective process.

The individual may, however, bring the power into manifestation and as the possible combinations of thought are infinite, the results are seen in an infinite variety of conditions and experiences.

Primordial man, naked and bestial, squatting in gloomy caverns and gnawing bones, was born, lived, and died in a hostile world. His hostility and his wretchedness arose from his ignorance. His handmaidens were Hate and Fear. His sole reliance was his club. He saw in the beasts, forests, torrents, seas, clouds, and even in his fellow man only enemies. He recognized no ties binding them one to another or to himself.

Modern man is born to comparative luxury. Love rocks his cradle and shields his youth. When he goes forth to struggle he wields a pencil, not a club. He relies upon his brain, not his brawn. He knows the physical as neither master nor equal, but as a useful servant. His fellow men and the forces of Nature are his friends, not his enemies.

These tremendous changes—from hate to love, from fear to confidence, from material strife to mental control, have been wrought by the slow dawn of Understanding. In direct proportion as he understands Cosmic Law is man's lot enviable or the reverse.

Thought builds organic structures in animals and men. The protoplasmic cell desires the light and sends forth its impulse; this impulse gradually builds an eye. A species of deer feed in a country where the leaves grow on high branches, and the constant reaching for their favorite food builds cell by cell the neck of the giraffe. The amphibian reptiles desire to fly in the open air above the water; they develop wings and become birds.

Experiments with parasites found on plants indicate that even the lowest order of life makes use of mental chemistry. Jacques Loeb[1], M.D., PH.D., a member of the Rockefeller Institute made the following experiment: "In order to obtain the material, potted rose bushes are brought into a room and placed in front of a closed window. If the plants are allowed to dry out, the aphides (parasites), previously wingless, change to winged insects. After the metamorphosis, the insects leave the plants, fly to the window, and then creep upward on the glass."

It is evident that these tiny insects found that the plants on which they had been thriving were dead and that they could therefore secure nothing more to eat and drink from this source. The only method by which they could save themselves from starvation was to grow temporary wings and fly, which they did.

That the brain cells are directly affected by mental pictures and that the brain cells in their turn can affect the entire being was proven by Prof. Elmer Gates[2] at the Smithsonian Institution at Washington. Guinea pigs were kept in enclosures with certain colors dominant; dissections showed their brains to be larger in the color area than those of the same class of guinea pigs kept in other enclosures. The perspiration of men in various mental moods was analyzed and the resultant salts experimented with. Those of a man in an angry state were of an unusual color; a small portion put on the tongue of a dog produced evidences of poisoning.

Experiments at Harvard College with students on the weighing board proved that the mind moves the blood. When the student was told to imagine that he was running a foot race, the board sank

---

1 Jacques Loeb (1859-1924) was a German physiologist used science to investigate the existence of free will. He held a mechanistic view of nature, believing that humans operated as a result of physical and chemical reactions to stimuli.

2 Elmer Gates believed that science, when it can sufficiently learn enough about the mind, could eventually put an end to crime.

down at the foot, and when a problem in mathematics was being worked, the balanced board sank down at the head.

This shows that thought not only flashes constantly between mind and body with an intensity and swiftness far transcending electricity, but that it also builds the structures through which it operates.

Through the conscious mind we know ourselves as individuals and take cognizance of the world about us. The subconscious mind is the storehouse of past thoughts.

We can understand the action of the conscious and subconscious minds by observing the process by which the child learns to play piano. He is taught how to hold his hands and strike the keys, but at first he finds it somewhat difficult to control the movement of his fingers. He must practice daily and must concentrate his thoughts upon his fingers, consciously making the right movements. These thoughts, in time, become subconscious—the fingers are directed and controlled in the playing by the subconscious. In his first months (and possibly first years of practice), the pupil can perform only by keeping his concentrated mind centered upon the work; but later he can play with ease and at the same time carry on a conversation with those around him, because the subconscious has become so thoroughly imbued with the idea of right movements that it can direct them without demanding the attention of the conscious mind.

The subconscious is instinctive desire. It carries out what is suggested by the conscious mind. These suggestions it carries out faithfully, and it is this close relation between the conscious and subconscious that makes conscious thinking so important.

Man's organism is controlled by the subconscious thought. Circulation, breathing, digestion, and assimilation are all activities controlled by the subconscious. The subconscious is continually getting its impulses from the conscious and we have only to change our conscious thought to get a corresponding change in the subconscious.

We live in a fathomless sea of plastic mind substance. This substance is ever alive and active. It is sensitive to the highest degree.

It takes form according to the mental demand. Thought forms the mold or matrix from which the substance expresses. Our ideal is the mold from which our future will emerge.

The Universe is alive. In order to express life, there must be mind; nothing can exist without mind. Everything that exists is some manifestation of this one basic substance from which and by which all things have been created and are continually being recreated. It is man's capacity to think that makes him a creator instead of a creature.

All things are the result of the thought process. Man has accomplished the seemingly impossible because he has refused to consider it impossible. By concentration, men have made the connection between the finite and the Infinite, the limited and the Unlimited, the visible and the Invisible, the personal and the Impersonal.

Great musicians have succeeded in thrilling the world by the creation of divine rhapsodies. Great inventors have made the connection and startled the world by their wonderful creations. Great authors, great philosophers, and great scientists have secured this harmony to such an extent that though their writings were created hundred of years ago, we are just beginning to realize their truths. Love of music, love of business, and love of creation caused these people to concentrate, and the ways and means of materializing their ideals slowly but surely developed.

Throughout the entire Universe, the law of cause and effect is ever at work. This law is supreme: Here a cause—there an effect. They can never operate independently. One is supplementary to the other. Nature at all times is endeavouring to establish a perfect equilibrium. This is the law of the Universe and it is ever active. Universal harmony is the goal for which all nature strives. The entire cosmos moves under this law. The sun, the moon, the stars are all held in their respective positions because of harmony. They travel their orbits, they appear at certain times in certain places, and because of the precision of this law, astronomers are able to tell us where various stars will appear in a thousand years. The scientist bases his entire hypothesis on this law of cause and effect. Nowhere is it held in dispute except in the domain of man. Here we find people speaking of luck, chance, accident, and mishap; but is any one of these possible? Is the Universe a unit? If so, and there is law and order in one part, it must extend throughout all parts. This is a scientific deduction.

Like begets like on every plane of existence, and while people believe this more or less vaguely, they refuse to give it any consideration where they are concerned. This is due to the fact that heretofore man could never realize how he set certain causes in motion that related to him with his various experiences.

It is only in the past few years that a working hypothesis could be formulated to apply this law to man—the goal of the Universe is harmony. This means a perfect balance between all things.

Ether fills all interplanetary space. This more or less metaphysical substance is the elementary basis of all matter. It is upon this substance that the messages of the wireless are transmitted through space.

Thought dropped into this substance causes vibrations, which in turn unite with similar vibrations and react upon the thinker. All manifestations are the result of thought, but the thinking is on different planes.

We have one plane of thought constituting the animal plane. Here are actions and interactions that animals respond to, yet men know nothing of. Then we have the conscious thought plane. Here are almost limitless planes of thought to which man may be responsive. It is strictly the nature of our thinking that determines to which plane we shall respond. On this plane, we have the thoughts of the ignorant, the wise, the poor, the wealthy, the sick, the healthy, the very poor, the very sick, and so on. The number of thought planes is infinite, but the point is that when we think on a definite plane, we are responsive to thoughts on that plane, and the effect of the reaction is apparent in our environment.

Take for example one who is thinking on the thought plane of wealth. He is inspired with an idea, and the result is success. It could not be otherwise. He is thinking on the success plane and as like attracts like, his thoughts attract other similar thoughts, all of which contribute to his success. His receiver is attuned for success thoughts only; all other messages fail to reach his consciousness;

hence, he knows nothing of them. His antennae, as it were, reach into the Universal Ether and connect with the ideas by which his plans and ambitions may be realized.

Sit right where you are, place an amplifier to your ear, and you may hear the most beautiful music, or a lecture, or the latest market reports. What does this indicate, in addition to the pleasure derived from the music or the information received from the lecture or market report?

It indicates first that there must be some substance sufficiently refined to carry these vibrations to every part of the world. Again it indicates that this substance must be sufficiently refined to penetrate every other substance known to man. The vibrations must penetrate wood, brick, stone, or steel of any kind. They must go over, through, and under rivers, mountains, above the earth, under the earth, everywhere and anywhere. Again it indicates that time and space have been annihilated. The instant a piece of music is broadcast in Pittsburgh or anywhere else, by putting the proper mechanism to your ear you can get it as clearly and distinctly as though you were in the same room. This indicates that these vibrations proceed in every direction. Wherever there is an ear to hear, it may hear.

If, then, there is a substance so refined that it will take up the human voice and send it in every direction so that every human being who is equipped with the proper mechanism may receive the message, is it not possible that the same substance will carry a thought just as readily and just as certainly? Most assuredly. How do we know this? By experimentation. This is the only way to be certain of anything. Try it. Make the experiment yourself.

Sit right where you are. Select a subject with which you are fairly familiar. Begin to think. The thoughts will follow each other in rapid succession. One thought will suggest another. You will soon be surprised at some of the thoughts that have made you a channel of their manifestation. You did not know that you knew so much about the subject. You did not know that you could put them into such beautiful language. You marvel at the ease and rapidity with which the thoughts arrive. Where do they come from? From the One Source of all wisdom, all power, and all understanding.

You have been to the source of all knowledge, for every thought which has ever been thought is still in existence, ready and waiting for someone to attach the mechanism by which it can find expression. You can there fore think the thoughts of every sage, every artist, every financier, every captain of industry who ever existed, for thoughts never die.

Suppose your experiment is not entirely successful. Try again! Few of us are proud of our first effort at anything. We did not even make a very great success in trying to walk the first time we tried. If you try again, remember that the brain is the organ of the objective mind, that it is related to the objective world by the cerebro-spinal or voluntary nervous system; that this system of nerves is connected with the objective world by a certain mechanism or senses. These are the organs with which we see, hear, feel, taste, and smell.

Now, a thought is a thing that can be neither seen nor heard—we cannot taste it, nor can we smell it, nor can we feel it. Evidently, the five senses can be of no possible value in trying to receive a thought. They must therefore be stilled, because thought is a spiritual activity and cannot reach us through any material channel. We will then relax both mentally and physically and send out an S.O.S. for help and await the results. The success of our experiment will then depend entirely upon our ability to become receptive.

Scientists like to make use of the word ether in speaking of the substance "in which we live and move and have our being," which is omnipresent, which impenetrates everything, and which is the source of all activity. They like to use the word Ether because Ether implies something which can be measured and so far as the materialistic school of scientists is concerned, anything which cannot be measured does not exist; but who can measure an electron? And yet the electron is the basis for all material existence, so far as we know at present.

It would require 500,000,000 atoms placed side by side to measure one linear inch. A number of atoms equal to twenty-five million times the population of the earth must be present in the test tube for a chemist to detect them in a chemical trace. About 125 septillions of atoms are in an inch cube of lead. And we cannot come anywhere near even seeing an atom through a microscope!

Yet the atom is as large as our solar system compared to the electrons of which it is composed. All atoms are alike in having one positive central sun of energy around which one or more negative charges of energy revolve. The number of negative electrons each atom contains determines the nature of the so-called "element" of which it is a part.

An atom of hydrogen, for instance, is supposed to have one negative electron as a satellite to its positive center. For this reason, chemists accept it as a standard of atomic weight. The atomic weight of hydrogen is placed at 1.

The diameter of an electron is to the diameter of the atom as the diameter of the Earth is to the diameter of the orbit in which it moves around the Sun. More specifically, it has been determined that an electron is one-eighteen-thousandth of the mass of a hydrogen atom.

It is clear therefore that matter is capable of a degree of refinement almost beyond the power of the human mind to calculate. We have not as yet been able to analyze this refinement beyond the electron, and even in getting thus far have had to supplement our physical observation of effects with imagination to cover certain gaps.

The building up of Matter from Electrons has been an involuntary process of individualizing intelligent energy.

Food, water, and air are usually considered to be the three essential elements necessary to sustain life. This is very true, but there is something still more essential. Every time we breathe, we not only fill our lungs with air that has been charged with magnetism by the Solar Orb, but we fill ourselves with Pranic Energy, the breath of life replete with every requirement for mind and spirit. This life-giving spirit is far more necessary than air, food, or water, because a man can live for forty days without food, for three days without water, and for a few minutes without air; but he cannot live a single second without Ether. It is the one prime essential of life and contains all the essentials of life, so that the process of breathing furnishes not only food for body building, but food for mind and spirit as well.

PART FOURTEEN

MENTAL MEDICINE

All that a man does outwardly is but the expression and completion of his inward thought. To work effectually, he must think clearly; to act nobly, he must think nobly. Intellectual force is a principle element of the soul's life, and should be proposed by every man as the principle of his being.

—Channing

MENTAL MEDICINE

In *The Law of Mental Medicine*, Thomas Jay Hudson says:

> Like all laws of nature, the law of mental medicine is universal in its application; and, like all the others, it is simple and easily comprehended.

Granted that there is an intelligence that controls the functions of the body in health, it follows that it is the same power or energy that fails in case of disease. Failing, it requires assistance; and that is what all therapeutic agencies aim to accomplish. No intelligent physician of any school claims to be able to do more than to "assist nature" to restore normal conditions of the body.

That it is a mental energy that thus requires assistance, no one denies; for science teaches us that the whole body is made up of a confederation of intelligent entities, each of which performs its functions with an intelligence exactly adapted to the performance of its special duties as a member of the confederacy. There is, indeed, no life without mind, from the lowest unicellular organism up to man. It is, therefore, a mental energy that actuates every fibre of the body under all conditions. That there is a central intelligence that controls each of those mind organisms is self-evident.

Whether, as the materialistic scientists insist, this central intelligence is merely the sum of all the cellular intelligences of the bodily organism, or is an independent entity, capable of sustaining a separate existence after the body perishes, is a question that does not concern us in the pursuance of the present inquiry. It is sufficient for us to know that such an intelligence exists and that, for the time being, it is the controlling energy that normally regulates the action of the myriad cells of which the body is composed.

It is, then, a mental organism that all therapeutic agencies are designed to energize, when, for any cause, it fails to perform its functions with reference to any part of the physical structure. It follows that mental therapeutic agencies are the primary and normal means of energizing the mental organism. That is to say, mental agencies operate more directly than any other, because more intelligibly, upon a mental organism; although physical agencies are by no means excluded, for all experience shows that a mental organism responds to physical as well as mental stimuli. All that can be reasonably claimed is that in therapeutics, mental stimulus is necessarily more direct and more positive in its effects, other things being equal, than a physical stimulus can be, for the simple reason that it is intelligent on the one hand and intelligible on the other. It must be remarked, however, that it is obviously impossible wholly to eliminate mental suggestion even in the administration of mental remedies. Extremists claim that the whole effect of material remedies is due to the factor of mental suggestion; but this seems to be untenable. The most that can be claimed with any degree of certainty is that material remedies, when they are not in themselves positively injurious, are good and legitimate forms of suggestions, and, as such, are invested with a certain therapeutic potency, as in the administration of the placebo. It is also certain that, whether the remedies are material or mental, they must, directly or indirectly, energize the mental organism in control of the bodily functions. Otherwise, the therapeutic effects produced cannot be permanent.

It follows that the therapeutic value of all remedial agencies, material or mental, is proportioned to their respective powers to produce the effect of stimulating the subjective mind to a state of normal activity and directing its energies into appropriate channels. We know that suggestion fills this requirement more directly and positively than any other known therapeutic agent; and this is all that needs to be done for the restoration of health in any case outside the domain of surgery. It is all that can be done. No power in the universe can do more than energize the mental organism that is the seat and source of health within the body. A miracle could do no more.

Professor Clouston, in his inaugural address to the Royal Medical Society in 1896, says:

> I would desire this evening to lay down or enforce a principle that is, I think, not sufficiently, and often not at all, considered in practical medicine and surgery. It is founded on a physiological basis and it is of the highest practical importance. The principle is that the brain cortex, and especially the mental cortex, has such a position in the economy that it has to be reckoned with more or less as a factor for good or evil in all diseases of every organ, in

> all operations, and in all injuries. Physiologically, the cortex is the great regulator of all functions, the ever-active controller of every organ disturbance. We know that every organ and every function are represented that they may be brought into the right relationship and harmony with each other, and so they all may be converted into a vital unity through it.
>
> Life and mind are the two factors of that organic unity that constitute a real animal organism. The mental cortex of man is the apex of the evolutionary pyramid, whose base is composed of the swarming pyramids of bacilli and other monocellular germs which we now see to be almost all-pervading in nature. It seems as if it has been the teleological aim of all evolution from the beginning. In it, every other organ and function find their organic end. In histological structure—so far as we know this—it far exceeds all other organs in complexity.
>
> When we fully know the structure of each neuron, with its hundreds of fibres and its thousands of dendrites, and the relation of one neuron to another, when we can demonstrate the cortical apparatus for universal intercommunication of nervous energy, with its absolute solidarity, its partial localization, and its wondrous arrangements for mind, motion, sensibility, nutrition, repair, and drainage—when we fully know all this, there will be no further question of the dominance of the brain cortex in the organic hierarchy, nor of its supreme importance in disease.

The Lancet records a case of Dr. Barkas of a woman (58) with supposed disease of every organ, with pains everywhere, who tried every method of cure, but was at last experimentally cured by mental therapeutics pure and simple. Assured that death would result from her state, and that a certain medicine would infallibly cure her, provided it was administered by an experienced nurse, one tablespoonful of pure distilled water was given her at 7, 12, 5, and

10, to the second with scrupulous care; and in less than three weeks all pain ceased, all diseases were cured, and remained so. This is a valuable experiment as excluding every material remedy whatever and proving that it is the mental factor alone that cures; however, it may be generally associated with material remedies.

Dr. Morrison of Edinburgh discovered that a lady who had constant violent hysterical attacks had given her hand to one man and her heart to another. A little direct common-sense talk in this case formed an agreeable substitute for the distilled water in the other, and the patient never had another attack.

Many seem to think only nervous of functional diseases are cured by Mental or Spiritual methods, but Alfred T. Schofield, M.D. tells in *The Force of Mind*:

> In one long list of 250 published cases of disease cured, we find five 'consumption,' one 'diseased hip,' five 'abscess,' three 'dyspepsia,' four 'internal complaint,' two 'throat ulcer,' seven 'nervous debility,' nine 'rheumatism,' five 'diseased heart,' two 'withered arm,' four 'bronchitis,' three 'cancer,' two 'paralyzed arm,' three 'weak eyes,' one 'ruptured spine,' five 'pains in the head.'

And these are the results in one year at one small chapel in the north of London.

What about the "cures" at home and Continental spas, with their eternal round of sulphur and iron waters and baths?

Does the doctor attached to the spa in his heart of hearts believe that all the cures which in these cases he cheerfully certifies to are effected by the waters, or even the waters and the diet, or even the waters and the diet and the air? Or does he not think there must be a "something else" as well? And to come nearer home and into the center of all things and the chamber of all his secrets: In his own consulting room and in his own practice, is not the physician brought face to face with cures and diseases, too, the cause of which he cannot account for? And is he not often surprised to find a continuation of the same treatment originated by the local practitioners is, when continued by his august self, efficacious? And is not the local practitioner not only surprised but disgusted as well to find such is the case?

Does any practical medical man, after all, really doubt these mental powers? Is he not aware of the ingredient "faith," which, if added to his prescriptions, makes them often all-powerful for good? Does he know experimentally the value of strongly asserting that the medicine will produce such and such effects as a powerful means of securing them?

If, then, this power is so well known, why in the name of common sense is it ignored? It has its laws of action, its limitations, its power for good and for evil. Would it not clearly help the medical student if these were indicated to him by his lawful teachers instead of his gleaning them uncertainly from the undoubted successes of the large army of irregulars?

We are, however, inclined to think that, after all, a silent revolution is slowly taking place in the minds of medical men, and that our present text books on disease, content with merely prescribing any mental cure in a single line as unworthy of serious consideration, will in time be replaced by others containing views more worthy of the century in which we live.

PART FIFTEEN

ORTHOBIOSIS

Every day that is born into the world comes like a burst of music and rings itself all the day through; and thou shalt make of it a dance, a dirge, or a life march as thou wilt.

—**Carlyle**

Virgil says, "Happy is he who has found the cause of things."

It was Metchnikoff[1] who tried, after his investigations into the physical, to apply ethics to life, so that life might be lived to the full, which is the true wisdom. He called this condition orthobiosis. He held that the end of science is to rid the world of its scourges through hygiene and other measures of prophylaxis.

Our manner of life, says Mme. Metchnikoff, transcribing her husband's ideas, will have to be modified and directed according to rational and scientific data of we are to run through the normal cycle of life—orthobiosis. The pursuit of that goal will ever influence the basis of morals. Orthobiosis cannot be accessible to all until knowledge, rectitude, and solidarity increase among men, and until social conditions are kinder.

Like all faculties, faith has a center through which it functions—the pineal gland. Faith is therefore physical, just as disease may be spiritual. Spirit and body are but parts of a glorious whole. The cure of disease requires the use of Cosmic Force; and who shall say that that force—whether we call it God, Nature, Oversoul, Brahma, *Vis Medicatrix Naturae*, *Prana*, Logos, or Divine Will—does not manifest itself through material means as well as spiritual?

"Plato," Dr. Butler tells us, "said that man is a plant rooted in heaven, and we agree to this, that he is also rooted in the earth." In fact, man may be said to have two origins, one earthly and physical, the other spiritual, though the former originates in the latter—so that ultimately the origin is one...

Man is an organism. De Quincey defines an organism as a group of parts which act upon the whole, the whole in turn acting upon all the parts. This is simple and true.

It is paradoxical that mind, though a principle and usually a determining part of a human organism's actions and reactions, has by formal medicine been disregarded as a primary cause in pretty much all of those bodily disorders that are not produced by contagion. But of late years autointoxication and disturbances of

1 Elie Metchnikoff (1845-1916) was a Russian biologist who worked on immunity in human beings.

the ductless glands have come into increased consideration. Their operations are being gradually traced to origins beyond the physical body, and definitely located in states of mind. These states are coming within the scope of diagnosis. Enlightened medical art brings them under treatment.

Recognition of the influence of mind upon the body was recognized even of old, as far back as Hippocrates and probably anterior to him. Mandeville, in the 14th century, approved of the custom of reciting certain verses of the psalms when taking medicine; nor was he averse to pilgrimages undertaken in search of health. He held that no harm could be done, while the potentialities of good were great. The value of the physical exercise in going on a pilgrimage, usually on foot with most of the time spent in the open air, need scarcely be pointed out. Many a cure of lethargy and obesity in the middle ages and after owed its efficacy to the insistence of famous physicians that the patients, no matter how wealthy or high-born, were to come from their dwellings on foot, in all humility, refusing to extend treatment otherwise.

Ignatius of Loyola[1] is credited with saying:

> Do everything you can with the idea that everything depends on you, and then hope for results just as if everything depended on God.

It will be found the sanest, most catholic and liberal exponents of each school of healing generously admit the value of other schools and the limitations of their own. The responsible healer of the future, who truly respects his honourable calling, will employ all beneficial, constructive agencies at the disposal of science. Thus, we have an eminent occultist[2] saying:

> In cases of misplacement, dislocation, or broken bones, the quickest way to obtain relief is to send for a competent physician or anatomist and have an adjustment made of the injured member or organ.

---

1 Ignatius of Loyola (1491-1556) was the principle founder of the Society of Jesus. He was canonized on March 12, 1622.

2 I could not discover who this occultist is. If you know, please contact Kallisti Publishing with the information. It will be appreciated.

> In cases of disruptions of blood vessels or muscles, a surgeon's aid should be immediately sought; not because mind is unable to cure any or all of these cases, but because of the fact that at the present time, even among educated people, mind is many times impotent through misuse or non-use. Mental treatment should follow these physical treatments in order to obviate unnecessary suffering and to obtain rapid recovery.

We cannot do better than to quote Sir William Osler[1], Bt., M.D., F.R.Sx.:

> The salvation of science lies in a recognition of a new philosophy—the *scientia scientiarum* of which Plato speaks: 'Now when all these studies reach the point of intercommunication and connection with one another and come to be considered in their mutual affinities, then, I think, and not until then, will the pursuit of them have a value.' (From *The Old Humanities and the New Science*)

Scientists assume that there is one substance only, and therefore their deduced science is the science of that substance and none other; and yet they are confronted with the fact that their one substance is differentiated, and that when they come to the finest degree thereof, as for instance bioplasm, they are brought face to face with the operation of higher laws than they are familiar with or can adequately explain.

Many scientists, however, with a broader view, are beginning to glimpse a "fourth dimension" and recognize the fact that there may be degrees of matter that are utterly beyond their chemical tests and microscopic lens.

But a new day is dawning. The telephone, the telegraph, and the wireless are now coming into general use and it is now possible to make use of every avenue of information and knowledge. It is therefore but a question of time when the sick will have the benefit

---

1 Sir William Osler (1849-1919) was a Canadian physician and is considered to be the Father of Modern Medicine.

of all that is known in the art of healing.

The physician frequently loses his patient because he refuses to recognize the spiritual nature of the patient, and that because of his spiritual nature there are certain fundamental laws governing in the spiritual world and that these laws continue to operate whether he recognizes them or not; and the metaphysician frequently loses his patient because he refuses to recognize that the body of the patient is the material manifestation of the spirit within, and the condition of the body is but an expression of the spirit.

But all this iconoclasm is but the result of a certain conservatism which is both human and natural. With the wisdom which the years are bringing, there will soon be no one who cannot see that the germ is not only the cause of disease, but the result of disease; that bacteria is the result of impure water not the cause of impure water; and so with everything else.

What we can see, handle, or touch are never causes, but always effects; and if it is our purpose to simply substitute one form of distress for another, we shall continue to deal with effects and effects only; but if it is our purpose to bring about a remedy, we shall seek the cause by which alone every effect is brought into existence, and this cause will never be found in the world of effects.

In the new era, abnormal mental and emotional conditions will be immediately detected and corrected. Tissue in process of destruction will be eliminated or reconstructed by the constructive methods at the disposal of the physician. Abnormal lesions will be corrected by manipulative treatment, but above and beyond all of this will be the primary and essential idea, the idea upon which all results will depend and that is that no inharmonious or destructive thought shall be allowed to reach the patient, that every thought for him and about him shall be constructive, for every physician, nurse, every attendant, every relative will eventually come to know that thoughts are spiritual things, which are ever seeking manifestation, and that as soon as they find fertile soil, they begin to germinate.

Not all thoughts find expression in the objective world and especially in the health and environment of the patient. This is because not all patients are responsive; but when the patient finds that these invisible guests come laden with precious gifts, they will be given a royal welcome. This welcome will be subconscious because the thoughts of others are received subconsciously.

The conscious mind receives thought only through the organs of perception, which are its method of contact with the objective world, which are the five senses—seeing, hearing, feeling, tasting, and smelling.

Subconscious thought is received by any organ of the body affected; and think of the mechanism which has been provided and which can and does objectify the thought received. First the millions of cell chemists ready and waiting to carry out all instructions received. Next, the complete system of communication, consisting of the vast sympathetic nervous system reaching every fiber of the being and ready to respond to the slightest emotion of joy or fear, of hope or despair, of courage or impotence.

Next, the complete manufacturing plant consisting of a series of glands wherein are manufactured all the secretions necessary for the use of the chemists in carrying out the instructions that have been given.

Then there is the complete digestive trait wherein food, water, and air are converted into blood, bone, skin, hair, and nails.

Then there is the supply department that constantly sends a supply of oxygen, nitrogen, and ether into every part of the being, and the wonder of it all is that this ether holds in solution everything necessary for the use of the chemist, for the ether holds in pure form, and food, water, and air in the secondary form, every element necessary for the use of the chemist in the production of a perfect man.

Why, then, do not these chemists produce a perfect specimen of manhood? The reply is simple: The prescriptions that consist of thoughts received by the subconscious call for nothing of the kind; in fact, they usually call for exactly the reverse.

The subconscious is also provided with a complete equipment for the elimination of waste and useless material as well as a complete repair department. In addition to this, there is a complete system of wireless whereby it is connected with every other subconscious entity in existence.

We are not usually conscious of the operation of this wireless, but the same thing is true concerning the operation of the Marconi System. There may be messages of all kinds all about us, but unless we make use of an amplifier, we receive no message, and so with our subconscious wireless. Unless we try to coordinate the conscious and the subconscious, we fail to realize that the subconscious is constantly receiving messages of some kind and just as constantly objectifying the messages in our life and environment.

This, then, is the mechanism devised and planned by the Creator Himself and it has been placed under the supervision of the subconscious instead of the conscious mind, but let us not forget that the subconscious mind with all of its wonderful mechanism can be controlled and dominated by the conscious mind when it becomes attuned to the Universal Mind, where all that is or ever was or ever shall be is held in solution waiting to come forth and manifest in form.

PART SIXTEEN

BIOCHEMISTRY

This above all: To thine own self be true,
And it must follow, as the night the day,
Thou canst not then be false to any man.

Biochemistry is a science whose concern is with vital processes and which has availed itself of the cell theory and of the principle of the infinite divisibility of matter. It also makes use of the homeopathic dose. The dose must be proportionate to the patient, the cell; for, as Virchow[1] has pointed out, "the essence of disease is the cell, changed pathogenically."

Dr. Schuessler, the originator of biochemistry, arrived at his conclusions by studying the elements, nature, and functions of human blood. The cells receive their substance, their life supply, from the blood and lymph, which, in their turn, derive their supply from the elements taken in as food. Normalcy in the supply of these elements means health; any deviation, a disturbance of health.

Dr. Schuessler placed the number of mineral combinations in the human body at twelve. In the last edition, 1895, he reduced the number to eleven. These all-necessary cell-salts are:

Potassium Chloride
Potassium Phosphate
Potassium Sulphate
Sodium Chloride
Sodium Phosphate
Sodium Sulphate
Phosphate of Lime
Fluoride of Lime
Phosphate of Magnesia
Phosphate of Iron
Silica

Milk contains all these elements; other foods can give them in combination. Cremation reduces the body to these elements.

Each kind of cell depends upon a different salt, or combination of salts, for its food; a lack of any of these salts is shown by certain symptoms. The proper tissue salts in right proportions are given to remove the symptoms, since a removal of the symptoms implies a removal of the need, or disease, in the cell.

---

1 Rudolf Ludwig Karl Virchow (1821-1902) was a German doctor who is credited with first recognizing leukemia. One of his most famous rules is "Every cell originates from another cell."

It must be remembered, however, that the cells are not fed, they feed themselves; and any attempt to compel them to accept more than they require causes disaster. They voluntarily accept what is necessary and they reject what they do not need.

The difference in the cells consists in the kind and quality of the inorganic tissue salts of which they are composed.

Health, therefore, requires the requisite quantity of cell-salts and a lack of some one of these organic tissue salts results in imperfect cell action and diseased tissue.

The controlling principle that underlies every manifestation of form may be epitomized as follows: "In the apportionment and grouping of the elements that constitute a thing lies the cause, not only of the form, but also of its functions and qualities."

Dr. Charles W. Littlefield, M.D., the author of *The Beginning and the Way of Life*, gives some very beautiful illustrations of the application of this law in the chapter on the "Elements and Compounds of Nature" in which he says:

"Within the scope and application of this principle of grouping electrons, as the law of origin of elements, molecules, tissues, organs, and forms, will be found a practical solution to every problem in biology from the origin and differentiation of species to every modification of form and configuration of outline that mark individuals with characteristic personalities, both physical and mental... It is well known in chemistry that the molecule is the smallest part of any substance that can exist separately and still retain its properties. Since the nature of the molecule is determined by the polarities, number, and arrangement of the 'electrons' that compose it, and since all structures in the mineral, vegetable, and animal kingdom are molecular, it follows that in the last analysis the grouping and apportionment of negative and positive 'electrons' in the molecule determine in turn the nature and physical conditions of the form, whether it be perfect or imperfect. Deformity, personal likes and dislikes, are only questions of being 'electronically' balanced or unbalanced, through supply or lack of supply of the forms of molecules that compose the organism. Only the spirit-mind-image of man, however, can make this grouping of molecules for the perfecting of a human form. To bring humanity to a state of primitive perfection, therefore, not only must the same material, prepared in the same manner, be supplied, but the environment of forces must be the same as those employed by the Creative Spirit in the beginning.

"Since then, we are able to trace every elemental form of matter back to some definite grouping of negative and positive electrons, that is, through varying numbers and arrangement of these; and since we find life manifesting through various forms as determined by different molecular groupings—by law of composition—and since it is rational to place Divine Mind behind this physical process, we are justified in assuming that Divine Mind-Images of living things preceded their physical development. Therefore, in the ultimate science of being, idealism is more probable than materialism. But, while mind may thus exist alone there in the realm of cause, here in the realm of phenomena we always have a psycho-physical parallelism, a realism, where everything must be explained by mind and matter, but by neither alone. While the spiritual entity which constitutes the real self may well be assumed to be akin to the Supreme Mind, being a particular mind-image thereof in the line of descent, having power of choice and therefore of independent action, it is unquestionably limited, like that of the player by his instrument, by bodily conditions."

In *The Chemistry of Life*, Dr. George W. Carey says:

"So-called disease is neither a person, place, nor thing."

The symptoms of sensation, called disease, are the results of lacking material—a deficiency in the dynamic molecules that carry on the orderly procedure of life. The effect of the deficiency causes unpleasant sensations, pains, exudations, swellings; or overheated tissue caused by increased motion of blood.

The increased motion is the effort nature, or chemical law, makes to restore equilibrium with the diminished molecules of blood builders. By the law of the conservation of energy, the increased motion is changed to heat. We call this effect fever.

Biochemistry means the *chemistry of life*, or the union of inorganic and organic substances whereby new compounds are formed.

In its relation to so-called disease, this system uses the inorganic salts, known as cell-salts, or tissue builders.

The constituent parts of man's body are perfect principles, namely oxygen, hydrogen, carbon, lime, iron, potash, soda, silica, magnesia, etc. These elements, gases, etc. are perfect per se, but may be endlessly diversified in combination as may the planks, bricks, or stones with which a building is to be erected.

Symptoms, called disease, disappear or cease to manifest when the food called for is furnished.

The human body is a receptacle for a storage battery and will always run right while the chemicals are present in proper quantity and combination, as surely as an automobile will run when charged and supplied with the necessary ingredients to vibrate or cause motion.

The cell-salts are found in all our food and are thus carried into the blood, where they carry on the process of life, and by the Law of Chemical Affinity keep the human form, bodily functions, materialized. When a deficiency occurs in any of these workers through a non-assimilation of food, poor action of liver, or digestive processes, dematerialization of the body commences. So, disease is a deficiency in some of the chemical constituents that carry on the chemistry of life.

Biochemists have shown that food does not form blood, but simply furnishes the mineral base by setting free the inorganic or cell-salts contained in all food stuff. The organic part—oil, fibrin, albumin, etc.—contained in food is burned or digested in the stomach and intestinal tract to furnish motive power to operate the human machine and draw air into lungs, thence into arteries, i.e., air carries.

Therefore, it is clearly proven that air unites with the minerals and forms blood, proving that the oil, albumin, etc., found in blood, is created every breath.

Increase the rate of activity of the brain cells by supplying more of the dynamic molecules of the blood known as mineral or cell-salts of lime, potash, sodium, iron, magnesia, silica, and we see mentally, truths that we could not sense at lower or natural rates of motion, although the lower rate may manifest ordinary health.

Natural man, or natural things, must be raised from the level of nature to supernatural, in order to realize new concepts that lie waiting for recognition.

By this regenerative process, millions of dormant cells of the brain are resurrected and set in operation, and then man no longer "sees through a glass darkly," but with the eye of spiritual understanding.

'Tis shown in Life's puzzles and sorrowings,
'Tis taught by remorse with its secret stings,
That he who grief to another brings,
One day, in his turn, must weep.

From the past doth the present eternally spring;
You may sow what you will, but tomorrow will bring
You the harvest, to show you the manner of thing
Is the seed you have chosen to sow!

PART SEVENTEEN

The NEW PSYCHOLOGY

The stars come nightly to the sky;
The tidal wave comes to the sea;
Nor time, nor space, nor deep, nor high
Can keep my own away from me.

—John Burroughs

The NEW PSYCHOLOGY

The observation and analysis, knowledge and classification of the activities of the personal consciousness, consisting of the science of psychology, has been studied in colleges and universities for many years, but this personal or conscious self-conscious mind does not by any means constitute the whole of the mind.

There are some very highly complex and very orderly activities going on within the body of an infant. The body of the infant, as such, cannot induce or carry on those activities, and the conscious mind of the infant does not know enough to even plan them or be aware of them. Probably also in most cases, there is no one around the infant who even remotely understands what is going on in this highly complex process of physical life; and yet all those activities manifest intelligence, and intelligence of a very complex and high order.

From the examination of what goes on in the human body, from all the complex processes, the beating of heart and digestion of food, the secretion and excretion of the glands, it is apparent that there is in control an order of mentality that has a higher degree of intelligence, but it is the mentality which is operating in the millions of cells that constitute the body, and so operate below the surface of what we term consciousness. It is therefore, subconscious.

The subconscious mind, again, assumes two phases. Connected with each human person there is a subconsciousness which may in some sense be regarded as the subconsciousness of that person, but which merges at a still deeper level into what may be termed Universal subconsciousness, or into cosmic consciousness. That may be illustrated in this way: If you will think of the waves on the surface of a lake, insofar as they are above the level of the troughs, as standing for so many personal mentalities; and then, if you will think of a small body of water not rising above the surface, but in some degree running along with each wave and merging indistinctly at the bottom into the great unmoved mass below, which may be thought of as the deepest level, then those three levels of the water in the lake may illustrate to you personal consciousness or self-consciousness, personal subconsciousness, and universal subconsciousness or cosmic consciousness. Now, out of cosmic consciousness springs personal subconsciousness, and out of that on turn, or in connection with it, rises personal consciousness.

At the beginning of the experience of the child, its government is almost wholly from subconsciousness; but as it goes on, it becomes aware maybe unconsciously, but still in a degree aware of the presence of laws of consciousness which manifest as justice, truthfulness, honesty, purity, liberty, loving-kindness, and so on, and begins to relate itself to them and to be governed by them more and more.

The first thing to note is that while this mental action is going on continuously, we are normally quite unconscious of it. For this reason, it is known as the subconscious department of the mind to distinguish it from the part which functions through the senses of which we are conscious, and which we call the self-conscious. The existence in the body of two distinct nervous systems—the cerebro-spinal and the sympathetic—each with its own field of operation and its special functions, prepared us for these two mental departments.

The cerebro-spinal system is used by the self-conscious and the sympathetic by the subconscious. And just as we find in the body that, while the functions and activities of the two nervous systems are different, provision has been made for very close interaction between the two, so we will find that, while the functions and activities of the two mental departments are different, there is a very definite line of activity between them.

The main business of the subconscious mind is to preserve the life and health of the individual. Consequently, it supervises all the automatic functions, such as circulation of the blood, the digestion, all automatic muscular action, and so on. It transforms food into suitable material for body building, returning it to conscious man in the form of energy.

Conscious man makes use of this energy in mental and physical work, and in the process uses up what has been provided for him by his subconscious intelligence.

The action of the subconscious is cumulative and may be illustrated in the following manner. Suppose you take a tub of water and begin to stir it with a small piece of wood from right to left with a circular motion. At first, you will start only a ripple around the wood, but if you keep the wood in motion with the circular movement, the water will gradually accumulate the strength that you are putting into the wood and presently you will have the whole tub of water in a whirl. If you were then to drop the piece of wood, the water would carry along the instrument that originally set it in motion, and if you were suddenly to stop the wood while it is still projecting in the water, there would be a strong tendency to not only carry the wood forward, but to take your hand along with it. Now, suppose that after you have the water whirling, you decide that you do not want it to whirl, or you think that you would prefer to have it whirl in the other direction, and so try to get it going the other way; you will find that there is great resistance and you will find that it will take a long while to bring the water to a standstill, and a still longer time before you get it going the other way.

This will illustrate that whatever the conscious mind does repeatedly the subconscious will accumulate as a habit. Any experience that the subconscious receives is stirred up and if you give it another one of the same kind it will add that to the former one and so keep on accumulating them indefinitely, the tendency being to accumulate activity along any definite line in increasing measure, and this holds true concerning any phase of activity that comes within range of human consciousness. This is true whether the experiences are for our benefit or otherwise, whether the experiences are good or evil. The subconscious is a spiritual activity and spirit is creative. The subconscious, therefore, creates the habits, condition, and environment that the conscious mind continues to entertain.

If we consciously entertain thoughts associated with art, music, and the aesthetic realm; if we consciously entertain thoughts associated with the good, the true, and the beautiful; then, we shall find these thoughts taking root in the subconsciousness and our experiences and environment will be a reflection of the thought which the conscious mind has entertained. If, however, we entertain thoughts of hatred, jealousy, envy, hypocrisy, disease, lack or limitation of any kind, then we shall find our experience and environment will reflect the conditions in accordance with these thoughts. "As we sow, so shall we reap." The law is no respecter of persons. We may think what we will, but the result of our thoughts is governed by an immutable law. "There is nothing good or evil, but thinking makes it so." We cannot plant seed of one kind and reap fruit of another.

Consciousness consists in the power to think, to will, and to choose; self-consciousness is the power to be aware of the self as a thinking, knowing, willing, and choosing individual. The brain is the organ of the conscious mind and the cerebro-spinal nervous system is the system of nerves by which it is connected with all parts of the body.

The process of growth is a subconscious process. We do not carry on the vital processes of nature consciously. All the complex processes of nature—the beating of the heart, the digestion of food, the secretion of the glands—require a high degree of mentality and intelligence. The personal consciousness or mind would not be capable of handling these intricate problems. They are, therefore, controlled by the Universal Mind, which in the individual we call the subconscious.

The Universal Mind is sometimes referred to as the Super-Conscious, and sometimes the Divine Mind. The subconscious is sometimes called the subjective and the conscious the objective mind, but remember that words are simply the vessels in which thought is carried. If you get the thought, you will not be concerned about the terms.

Mind is a spiritual activity and spirit is creative, hence the subconscious mind not only controls all the vital functions and processes of growth, but is the seat of memory and habit.

The sympathetic nervous system is the instrument by which the subconscious keeps in touch with the feeling or emotions, thus the subconscious reacts to the emotions, never to the reason, as the emotions are much stronger than the reason or intellect. The individual will therefore frequently act in exactly the opposite manner from what the reason and intellect would dictate.

It is axiomatic that two things cannot occupy the same space at the same time. What is true of things is true of thoughts. If, therefore, any thought seeks entrance to the mental realm which is destructive in its nature, it should be quickly displaced by a thought that has a constructive tendency. Herein lies the value of a ready made affirmation, such as the Coue affirmation:

> **Day by day, in every way, I am growing better and better.**

Or the Andrews affirmation:

> **I am whole, strong, powerful, loving, harmonious, and happy.**

These or similar affirmations may be committed to memory and repeated until they become automatic or subconscious. As physical conditions are but the outward manifestations of mental conditions, it will readily be seen that by constantly holding the thought expressed in the affirmation in the mind, that it will be but a comparatively short time until conditions and environment begin to change so as to be in accordance with the new method of thinking.

This same principle can be brought into operation in a negative way, though, through the process of denial. Many make use of this with excellent results.

The conscious and subconscious are but two phases of action in connection with the mind. The relation of the subconscious to the conscious is quite analogous to that existing between a weather vane and the atmosphere. Just as the least pressure of the atmosphere causes an action on the part of the weather vane, so does the least thought entertained by the conscious mind produce within the subconscious mind action in exact proportion to the depth of feeling characterizing the thought and the intensity with which the thought is indulged.

It follows that if you deny unsatisfactory conditions, you are withdrawing the creative power of your thought from these conditions. You are cutting them away at the root. You are sapping their vitality.

The law of growth necessarily governs every manifestation in the objective, so that a denial of unsatisfactory conditions will not bring about instant change. A plant will remain visible for some time after its roots have been cut, but it will gradually fade away and eventually disappear, so the withdrawal of your thought from the contemplation of unsatisfactory conditions will gradually but surely terminate these conditions.

This is exactly an opposite course from the one that we would normally be inclined to adopt. It will therefore have an exact opposite effect to the one usually secured. Most persons concentrate upon unsatisfactory conditions, thereby giving the condition that measure of energy and vitality that is necessary in order to supply a vigorous growth.

> The possibilities of thought training are infinite, its consequence eternal, and yet few take the pains to direct their thinking into channels that will do them good, but instead leave all to chance, or, rather, to the myriad of circumstances that buffet and compel our mental action if counter effort is not made.
>
> —**Marden**

PART EIGHTEEN

SUGGESTION

All truly wise thoughts have been thought already thousands of times; but to make them truly ours, we must think them over again honestly, 'til they take root in our personal experience.

—Goethe

Mr. C. Harry Brooks tells of a very interesting and instructive visit to the clinic of Dr. Emile Coue in a book entitled *The Practice of Auto-Suggestion*, published by Dodd, Mead & Co. The clinic is situated in a pleasant garden attached to Dr. Coue's house at the end of the rue Jeanne d'Arc, in Nancy. He states that when he arrived, the room reserved for patients was already crowded, but in spite of that, eager newcomers constantly tried to gain entrance. The window sills on the ground floor were beset and a dense knot had formed in the door. The patients had occupied every available seat and were sitting on camp stools and folding chairs.

He then tells of the many remarkable cures which Dr. Coue proceeded to effect by no other means than suggestion to the patient that the power of healing lies within the patient himself. There was also a children's clinic in charge of Mademoiselle Kauffmant who devotes her entire time to this work.

Mr. Brooks thinks that Coue's discoveries may profoundly affect our life and education because it teaches us that the burdens of life are, at least in a large measure, of our own creating. We reproduce in ourselves and in our circumstances the thoughts in our minds. It goes further, it offers us a means by which we can change these thoughts when they are evil and foster them when they are good, so producing a corresponding betterment in our individual life. But the process does not end with the individual. The thoughts of society are realized in social conditions, the thoughts of humanity in world conditions. What would be the attitude towards our social and international problems of a generation nurtured from infancy in the knowledge and practice of auto-suggestion? If each person found happiness in his own heart, would the illusory greed for possession survive? The acceptance of auto-suggestion entails a change of attitude, a revaluation of life. If we stand with our faces westward we see nothing but clouds and darkness, yet by a simple turn of the head, we bring the wide panorama of the sunrise into view.

The New York Times, under date of August 6, 1922, published and excellent likeness of Emile Coue and a review of his work by Van Buren Thorne, M.D. He says that the keynote to the system of treatment of mental and physical ills devised and elaborated by

Emile Coue of Nancy, France, can be described in a single paragraph:

> The individual is possessed of two minds called the conscious and the unconscious. The latter is referred to by some psychologists as the subconscious mind, and is literally the humble and obedient servant of the conscious mind. The unconscious mind is the director and overseer of our internal economy. By means of its activities, the processes of digestion and assimilation of foods are carried on, repairs are made, wastes are eliminated, our vital organs function, and life itself persists. When the thought arises in the conscious mind that extra efforts toward the repair of some deficiency, either physical or mental, are needed, all the individual has to do, in the opinion of Dr. Coue, is audibly to enunciate that thought in the form of a direct suggestion to the unconscious mind, and that humble obedient servant immediately, and without questioning the dictates of its conscious master, proceeds to obey instructions.

Dr. Coue, Mr. Brooks, and large numbers of persons of repute in France, England, and elsewhere in Europe, have declared that the results in many cases under their direct observation have been nothing short of marvelous. Those who have not witnessed the benefits of this form of treatment—hence may incline to be skeptical—are more likely to give attention to what follows when they are informed of three facts regarding the Nancy practice.

First, Dr. Coue has never accepted a penny for his treatments in the many years of his ministration.

Second, he is in the habit of explaining to his patients that he possesses no healing powers, has never healed a person in his life, and that they must find the instrument of their own well-being in themselves.

Third, that any individual can treat himself without consulting any other person.

It may be added that a child who is capable of comprehending the fact of the conscious and subconscious mind and is competent to issue orders from one to the other is quite capable of the self-administration of the treatment.

> For what man knoweth the things of a man save the spirit of the man which is in him?

Mr. Brooks quotes from First Corinthians for his title page. Doubtless this was selected as an apt biblical reference to the existence of the conscious and unconscious minds. But neither the treatment, nor this book about it, dwells at length upon any possible religious significance of the methods employed or the results obtained.

The single thing that has contributed largely to the recent rapid spread of knowledge concerning Dr. Coue's method of practice at Nancy is his insistence upon the benefits to be derived from the frequent repetition of this formula:

> **Day by day, in every way, I'm getting better and better.**

As I remarked, no great stress is laid upon the religious significance of his alleged cures; yet, says Mr. Brooks, "religious minds who wish to associate the formula with God's care and protection might do so after this fashion: 'Day by day, in every way, by the help of God, I'm getting better and better.'"

The secret of success in the treatment is to so beget confidence in the conscious mind that what it repeats is accepted at its face value by the unconscious mind, and as Mr. Brooks puts it:

> Every idea which enters the conscious mind, if it is accepted by the unconscious, is transformed by it into a reality and forms henceforth a permanent element in our life.

But let us see how this book came to be written, and then watch Dr. Coue at work.

Mr. Brooks is an Englishman who became interested in Dr. Coue's work at Nancy and went there to observe it at first hand. In his foreword to the volume, Dr. Coue says that Mr. Brooks visited him for several weeks last summer, and that he was the first Englishman who came to Nancy with the express purpose of studying methods of conscious auto-suggestion. He attended Dr. Coue's consultations and obtained a full mastery of the method. Then the two men threshed out a good deal of the theory on which the treatment rests.

Dr. Coue says that Mr. Brooks skillfully seized on the essentials and that he has put them forward in the volume in a manner that seems to him both simple and clear.

"It is a method," says Dr. Coue, "which every one should follow—the sick to obtain healing, the healthy to prevent the coming of disease in the future. By its practice we can insure for ourselves, all our lives long, an excellent state of health, both of the mind and the body."

Now let us enter Dr. Coue's clinic with Mr. Brooks. Back of the house there is a pleasant garden with flowers, strawberry beds, and fruit-laden trees. Groups of patients occupy the garden seats. There are two brick buildings—the waiting and consultation rooms. These are crowded with patients—men, women, and children.

Coue immediately proceeds to his work. Patient No. 1 is a man of middle age and frail. He can scarcely walk and his head, legs, and arms shake with an exaggerated tremor. His daughter supports him. Coue invites him to arise and walk. Aided by a stick, he staggers across the floor a few steps.

Coue tells him he is going to get better and adds, "You have been sowing bad seeds in your Unconscious; now you will sow good seed. The power by which you have produced such ill effects will in the future produce equally good ones."

"Madame," he tells a woman who breaks into a torrent of complaint, "you think too much about your ailments, and in thinking of them you create fresh ones."

He tells a girl with headaches, a youth with inflamed eyes, and a laborer with varicose veins, that auto-suggestion should bring complete relief. He comes to a neurasthenic girl who is making her third visit to the clinic and who has been practicing the method at home for ten days. She says she is getting better. She can now eat heartily, sleep soundly, and is beginning to enjoy life.

A big peasant, formerly a blacksmith, next engages his attention. He says he has not been able to raise his right arm above the level of his shoulder for nearly ten years. Coue predicts a complete cure. For forty minutes he keeps on with the interrogation of patients.

Then he pays attention to those who have come to tell him of the benefits they have received. Here is a woman who has had a painful swelling in her breast, diagnosed by the doctor (in Coue's opinion wrongly) as cancerous. She says that with three weeks' treatment, she has completely recovered. Another has overcome her anaemia and has gained nine pounds in weight. A third says he has been cured of varicose ulcer. While a fourth, a lifelong stammerer, announces a complete cure in one sitting.

Coue now turns to the former blacksmith and says, "For ten years you have been thinking you could not life your arm above your shoulder; consequently, you have not been able to do so, for whatever we think becomes true for us. Now think: 'I can lift it.'"

The man looks doubtful, says half-heartedly, "I can," makes an effort, and says it hurts.

"Keep it up," Coue commands in a tone of authority, "and think 'I can, I can!' Close your eyes and repeat with me as fast as you can, 'ça passe, ça passe.'"After half a minute of this, Coue says, "Now think well that you can lift your arm."

"I can," says the man with conviction and proceeds to raise it to full height, where he holds it in triumph for all to see.

"My friend," observes Dr. Coue quietly, "you are cured."

"It is marvelous," says the bewildered blacksmith. "I believe it."

"Prove it," says Coue, "by hitting me on the shoulder." Whereupon the blows fall in regular sequence.

"Enough," cautions Coue, wincing from the sledge-hammer blows. "Now you can go back to your anvil."

Now he turns to Patient No. 1, the tottering man. The sufferer seems inspired with confidence by what he has seen. Under Coue's instructions, he takes control of himself and in a few minutes he is walking about with ease.

"When I get through with the clinic," says Coue, "you shall come for a run in the garden."

And so it happens. Very soon this patient is trotting around the enclosure at five miles per hour.

Coue then proceeds to the formulation of specific suggestions. The patients close their eyes and he speaks in a low, monotonous voice. Here is an example:

"Say to yourself that all the words I am about to utter will be fixed, imprinted, and engraved in your minds; that they will remain fixed, imprinted, and engraven there, so that without your will and knowledge, without your being in any way aware of what is taking place, you yourself and your whole organism will obey them. I tell you first that every day, three times a day, morning, noon, and evening, at meal times, you will be hungry; that is to say, you will feel the pleasant sensation which makes us think and say: 'How I should like something to eat.' You will then eat with an excellent appetite, enjoying your food, but you will never eat too much. You will eat the right amount, neither too much nor too little, and you will know intuitively when you have sufficient. You will masticate your food thoroughly, transforming it into a smooth paste before swallowing it. In these conditions you will digest it well, and so feel no discomfort of any kind either in the stomach or in the intestines. Assimilation will be perfectly performed, and your organism will make the best possible use of the food to create blood, muscle, strength, energy—in a word, Life."

"They (Dr. Coue and Mlle. Kauffmant)," says Mr. Brooks, "have placed not only their private means, but their whole life at the service of others. Neither ever accepts a penny-piece for the treatments they give, but I have never seen Coue refuse to give a treatment at however awkward an hour the subject may have asked for it. The fame of the school has now spread to all parts, not only France, but of Europe and America. Coue's work has assumed such proportions that his time is taken up often to the extent of fifteen or sixteen hours a day. He is a living monument to the efficacy of 'Induced Auto-suggestion.'"

In *Regeneration*, Mr. Weltmer says:

"The last battle in which the race is engaged is now on. It is not a battle of cannon and sword, but it is a conflict of ideas. It is not going to be destructive, but constructive. It will not be a destroying warfare, but a fulfilling. It will not promote discord, but will insure harmony. It will not knit the human family together in combinations and associations, lodges, and congregations, but will individualize the race, and each person will stand alone, recognizing within himself all the potentialities that exist, recognizing within himself all the Divine principles constituting a part of the perfect whole.

"When man see himself thus, he will see this kingdom within not is not within him only but within all men. We must assume that the power to do, to act, or to perform the work we give our minds to do, exists in the mind; but before we entrust the mind with this work, we must have a clear conception of what is to be done. In order to regenerate the body, we must conclude or assume to be true that the power to generate life and health is in us; we must know where it is generated and how to generate it.

"Could we but comprehend it, could the veil of ignorance that enshrouds us be lifted, and we be allowed to look into the storehouse of knowledge, such as the prophet or seer was allowed to look upon, could we but climb where Moses stood, and view the landscape o'er, could we experience what Paul did during the time when he says 'I know not whether I was in the body or out of the body,' we would be able to comprehend what he means when he says 'Eye hath not seen, nor ear heard, nor hath it entered into the heart of man, the glory that shall be revealed in us.'"

The brain is an organ through which we communicate our thoughts to other organs in our bodies and receive impressions from the outside through the mediums of the senses. Great men have by great thoughts developed a finer quality of brain than others; this leads people to think that the great mind was the outgrowth of the fine brain, when if they will look upon the brain as any other organ of the perishable body, they will see that it is but the organ through which the mind finds expression.

All attainments come in their regular order, as orderly as the movements of the sun and planets; first we desire, second we believe, third we try the belief, fourth we have knowledge.

We entertain a belief and the belief comes into our minds and controls us. A man in the throes of poverty can throw off the shackles, if he can add to his belief.

A suggestion, to be a controlling influence, must be a positive suggestion left undisturbed. It must be regarded by the person entertaining it as a fixture in his life, not subject to change or modification.

Still another method of making an application of the principle of suggestion is described by Mr. J.R. Seaward, of Hamilton, Mont. He says:

"I am a man of 36 years of age and have a family, and they rejoice with me that I am free from the use of tobacco. I chewed, or rather ate, the weed for 15 years. Didn't mean to form the habit when I started in, but thought that it was conducive to my growth from youth to manhood. After the habit had grown on me for several years unresisted, I discovered that I was in the grip of a slowly, but surely, growing octopus that had me freely within its embrace, and I was helpless to release myself. I had followed carpenter and shop woodwork for a trade, and all woodworkers know there is something about lumber that makes a man want to use tobacco. When I got so that I had to chew all the time and the strongest I could get and then was not satisfied, I began to wonder where I was headed for. Slowly, the idea that I was a slave to the weed dawned on me and I began to think about cutting down on it, or out altogether.

"I will now explain to you the way in which Friend Wife broke me of a vile habit and convinced us both of the marvelous power of Suggestion when properly applied.

"At about the time that I struck bottom, there came to my notice some literature telling of the power of directed thought, and I became interested in the study of that, and also in some inspirational literature which later came to my notice. I was rather skeptical at first, but as I read and thought and commenced to look for proof in the events of our daily lives and in our environment, the truth commenced to dawn upon me. I began to see and know that life manifestations were fed from within and grew from within, and if the within be in a state of decay, it invariably showed without. In fact, I know now that 'The Man of Galilee' said something when He said, 'As a man thinketh in his heart, so is he.' If he thinks himself a slave to tobacco or other obnoxious habits, so is he. He must think himself free to remain free, once he has gained freedom.

"But to think one's self away from a habit that clings as close as thought itself is a hard matter unaided. At the time we tried suggestion for the elimination of my tobacco habit, I slept in one bedroom with one of the children and my wife slept in another bedroom with our then youngest boy, about eight months old. As often is the case, she had to be up at times during the night to wait on the baby and it was at those times that she gave me mental treatments while I was asleep.

"It isn't necessary to be in the same room, though it is all right if it happens to be the case. While I was sleeping, she would visualize herself or mentally project herself as though she was standing of kneeling beside my bed and speaking to me. Her suggestions were of a constructive and positive nature rather than of negative. It went something like this: 'You are now desiring freedom from the tobacco habit; you are free and desire and enjoy mastery more than indulgence; tomorrow you will want only about half the normal amount of tobacco and each day it will be less until you are free within a week and shall never have any more craving for tobacco. You are Master and free.'

"She made the above suggestion (in substance) to me each time that she was awake during the night and I do pledge on oath that within six days from the time she started treatment, I had completely quit craving tobacco and quit using it. That has been several months ago, and today I am more master of my habits of thought and word and deed than ever before in my life. I have changed from an under-weight, nervous wreck to a full-weight, healthful, strong, energetic, and clear-thinking man, and everyone who knew me remarks how differently I look and act and seem. Since that time, I have followed the study and the practice of constructive and directed thinking."

You know that in wireless telegraphy or telephony they use an instrument called the tuning coil that vibrates in harmony with an electrical wave or vibration of a certain length. It is in tune with that particular tune of wave and consequently they are in harmony and allow the vibration to go on to the other receiving instrument unhindered. Yet there may be other wireless vibrations of a higher or lower "tune" or key passing at the same time, yet only those in harmony are registered by the receiver.

Now, our minds are just about the same way, only we regulate our "tuning coil" by our mind. We can "tune" our minds to low-vibration thoughts such as the animal impulses of nature, or we can "tune" them to thoughts of an educational or mental nature, or we can (after some qualifications are met) "tune" ourselves to receive purely spiritual thought vibrations. This power constitutes the Divine power that is given to man. Of course you will readily see that there never was a primitive hut or modern mansion built without the application of this principle of directed constructive thinking and visualization.

The backbone of salesmanship of all kinds is the understanding and skillful use of suggestion. When cleverly used, it tends to relax one's conscious attention and warm up and quicken the Desire until a favorable response is gained. Window displays and counter displays as well as illustrated advertising all rely on the power to drive a suggestion in the very center of Desire, where it grows to the point of action if in harmony with the thought vibration of the Desire. If the desire does not recognize or is not in harmony with the suggestion, it is as "seed that has fallen upon stony ground," and is without harvest of action.

Thought and action do produce material results as is easily verified in the builder and his plans, the dressmaker and her patterns, or the school and it product—all in harmony with the leading constructive thought. The quality of thought determines the measure of success in life.

PART NINETEEN

PSYCHO-ANALYSIS

He has achieved success who has lived well, laughed often, and loved much; who has gained the trust of pure women and the love of little children; who has filled his niche and accomplished his tasks; who has left the world better than he found it; who has never lacked appreciation of earth's beauties or failed to express it; who has always looked for the best in others and given the best he had; whose life was an inspiration, whose memory a benediction.

—B.A. Stanley

PSYCHO-ANALYSIS

"Canst thou not minister to a mind diseased," asked Macbeth of the Doctor—but the passage is so strikingly fitting, so prophetically explanatory of psycho-analysis, that it must be given in full:

> Macbeth: Canst thou not minister to a mind diseased,
> Pluck from the memory a rooted sorrow,
> Raze out the written troubles of the brain,
> And with some sweet oblivious antidote
> Cleanse the stuff'd bosom of that perilous stuff
> Which weighs upon the heart?
>
> Doctor: Therein the patient must minister to himself.

There is hardly a person today exempt from some form of phobia, or fear, whose origin may date so far back as to be lost among the shadows of childhood. Hardly a person is free from some aversion, or "complex," whose effects are a matter of daily occurrence, despite the will of the victim. In a sense, the subconsciousness has never forgotten the incident and still harbors the unpleasant memory of it. The consciousness, however, in an attempt to protect our dignity or vanity, whichever you prefer, may evolve some apparent, better reason than the original one. Thus, complexes are formed. Brontephobia, or fear of thunder, was brought about in the case of one patient by hearing a cannon go off very near her when she was a child, a fact that had been "forgotten" for years. To confess to such a fear, even to one's self, would have been childish—and fear to the somewhat more dignified cause of thunder. Needless to say, it is such disguises of the memories that make difficult the labor of the psycho-analyst to pluck from the memory a rooted sorrow, to raze out the written troubles of the brain, its "traumas" or the original shocks. And when we remember that Psyche in Greek means not only the mind but the soul, we can better understand Shakespeare's amazing grasp of psychology when he speaks not only of the "mind diseased," but of "that perilous stuff which weighs upon the heart."

We all have these complexes, in forms ranging from the mild to the severe: sitophobia, the aversion to certain foods; claustrophobia, the fear of locked doors—to which the fear of open spaces forms a striking contrast; stage-fright; touching wood and other superstitions... A thorough list would indeed be a very long one.

For the greater part, the patient must minister to himself—with the help of the skilled psycho-analyst. In some cases, elaborate process are needed, and the use of psychometers and other delicate registering devices enlisted; but usually, the procedure is a simple one. The subject of investigation is made comfortable physically and put in a quiet mood; he is then told to utter whatever may come into his mind in connection with his complex—with occasional promptings and questions from the psycho-analyst. Sooner or later the association of ideas will bring to the surface the original cause or experience that had become "rooted" or submerged. Very often, the mere explanation will suffice to eradicate the obsession.

But there is another group of disorders, hysteria, which may partake both of the physical and the psychical, or where either state may induce the other. Richard Ingalese in his *History and Power of Mind*[1] has summed up the matter very clearly: "Disease may be divided into two classes, the imaginary and the real. Imaginary disease is a picture held firmly by the objective mind, which causes more or less physical correspondence. This kind of disease is often created in total disregard of the laws governing anatomy or physiology; and is the hardest to cure, because persons possessed of it hold to it so persistently that an entire revision of their mode of thought must be made before it can be cured. It is not at all infrequent to have a patient complain of kidney disease, locating the pain and the organs several inches below the waist line. The spleen is often supposed to be in the right side of the body, and phantom tumors appear and disappear. But all these mental pictures, if held long enough, create matrices or vortices, and draw into them the elements that will bring finally the actual disease that was at first purely imaginary."

Psycho-analysis proceeds upon the assumption that a very large number of cases of disease are caused by repression of normal desires, or by disturbances that have occurred in the past life of the individual. In such cases, the root of the disease is so concealed,

---

1 Richard Ingalese (1854-?) was, with his wife Isabella, a New Thoughter and alchemist.

sometimes through years and years, that it must be searched for.

The psycho-analyst is enabled to locate such difficulties through dreams, or rather through the interpretation of dreams, or by questioning the patient concerning his past life. The well-trained analyst must of necessity secure the friendly confidence of the patient to such an extent that the latter will not hesitate to reveal any experience, no matter how intimate.

As soon as the patient has been led to remember a particular experience, he is encouraged to talk about it in detail and thus it is brought up from subconsciousness. The analyst then shows him what has been causing the difficulty, and when the cause is eradicated it can do no more harm.

It is exactly parallel to a foreign substance in the flesh: There is a horrible swelling with inflammation, pain, and suffering; the surgeon is called; he removes the difficulty and nature does the rest. The psychological law follows the same procedure. If there has been any abnormal activity—any festering sore in the subconscious mind going on for years and years—if it can be located by a process of mental analysis and put out of the mental complex and shown to the patient, the catharsis is complete.

Dr. Hugh T. Patrick, clinical professor of nerves and mental disease in Northwestern University Medical School, mentions several interesting cases.

"In many cases of functional nervous disorders, the factor of fear is quite obvious. But in many cases, though equally important, it is not at once apparent. Of the latter, there are numerous varieties which may be divided into groups. One group embraces patients known to have physical courage. A few years ago, there was referred to me one of the most noted as well as fearless en in the ring, a man who was particularly carefree, if not careless. He was suffering with what were considered rather vague and baffling nervous symptoms, principally insomnia, lack of interest, and moodiness. A careful analysis soon revealed that some trifling symptoms, due to high living and domestic friction, had served to put the idea into his head that he was losing his mind. This phobia was sickness, and the fear so possessed his soul that he was good for nothing until he got rid of it. Needless to say, the patient himself was quite unconscious of the nature of his trouble, and his physician had overlooked it."

So they could not cure the trouble from a physical standpoint. The situation had to be mentally analyzed, and the cause of the fear dragged out from subconsciousness and exposed to the man. When he had a look at it, it had exactly the same effect as pulling an eyelash out from an inflamed eye and letting you see it. Your troubles are all over right away, because you are very sure the disturbing cause has been removed, and you forget about it then.

"A sheep rancher of Wyoming complained of insomnia, loss of appetite, abdominal distress, general nervousness, and inability to look after his ranch. What really was the matter with him was fear of cancer of the stomach. This phobia completely unnerved him and caused him to enormously magnify every bodily sensation. But was he a nerveless coward? Decidedly not. There was a time when the cattlemen of the Far West made sheep raising a hazardous occupation. Through these dangerous years, he lived without a tremor, though he never went to sleep without a rifle by his side. Once, he was informed that three cattlemen had started out to 'get him,' and the information was correct. He mounted his horse and, properly armed, rode out to meet them. As he expressed it, he 'talked them out of it,' and the three would-be assassins turned and rode away. In this encounter he was not in the least apprehensive or uncomfortable, and I learned of the incident only in a conversation about his business."

He had plenty of physical courage, but when something in the inner organism seemed to be wrong, he was scared. As soon as this doctor discovered what the fear was, he probably produced an X-ray or something of that nature to show the patient that there was nothing the matter. Then, drawing the patient's attention to the groundless fear, the doctor was able to convince the patient of the groundlessness of his fears.

"A policeman, 49 years old, suffered from intractable insomnia, head pressure, general nervousness, and loss of weight. He was not a man to suspect of fear. For many years he had been in active service in one of the worst precincts of Chicago, and on account of his familiarity with criminals was frequently sent after the worst types. He had been in numerous 'gun' fights. Once, a notorious 'gunman' standing beside him fired point blank at his head. All this disturbed his equanimity not a whit. And yet his illness was the result of fear pure and simple. It came about in this way: a malicious person had preferred against him charges of misconduct and he was cited to appear before the trial board. This worried him greatly. Innocent, he keenly felt the disgrace of the accusation and feared that he might be suspended or even discharged. He trembled for his well-earned good name and for his home, on which there was a mortgage. Naturally, he began to sleep poorly, to have queer feelings in his head, and then to feel uncertain of himself. At this juncture, some friends sympathetically told him that one could go insane from worry. These were the steps: Fear of disgrace; fear of financial collapse; fear of insanity. But did the patient know all this? Not he. He knew only that he was nervous and that he suffered and that he did not feel sure of himself."

When that was dragged out of his consciousness and shown to him as a root of his trouble and a physician was able to assure him that fear was all in the world that was the matter with him, he made up his mind that he had better give that up. Then he was healed.

The subconscious mentality is sick in a chronic was. It has been made sick by some kind of mental experience—usually of many years' standing—and the sickness is a result of its continuing to cherish that experience and keeping it before itself. This constitutes what is technically called a "running sore" in the subconscious—that is, mentally not physically.

A woman had suffered from general debility for a number of years and had been unable to secure relief. The psychologist began to probe to see what the trouble was. He began to pronounce words—just anything that came into his thoughts: "Desk, book, rug, Chinaman." When he pronounced the word "Chinaman", the woman appeared startled. He then asked her what the word "Chinaman" suggested to her and why it startled her. The woman said that when she was a little girl, she and a playmate used to play around a Chinese laundry and that they used to plague the Chinaman by throwing pebbles at him through the open door; one day the Chinaman chased them with a big knife and they were nearly scared to death. "Yes," said the psychologist, "that is one of the things that I wanted to know." Then he began to pronounce more words, presently the word "water" and again the woman was startled. It developed then that one time when she was a very little girl, she and her brother were playing on the wharf and that accidentally she pushed him into the water and he was drowned. She said it was many years ago, when she was a mere child. The psychologist asked, "Do you think of these things very often?" She said, "No, I do not know that I have thought of them before in fifteen or twenty years." "Well," he said, "I will tell you what I want you to do." (She was at that time in a sanitarium under the care of a nurse.) "I want you to tell the nurse every day that experience about the Chinaman and also the experience about your brother, and I want you to keep telling it until you have told it so many times that you do not feel bad about it any more; then, see me again in two or three weeks." She did as he directed, and at the end of sixty days she was well. The effect of telling it so often was its becoming commonplace to the conscious mentality, without touching the feelings. So the suggestion then went down to the subconsciousness that it did not feel badly about the incident any more, and the conditions of fear which had persisted for twenty or twenty-five years were erased and the complex in the subconsciousness was no longer in evidence.

The subconscious mind has perfect memory and is fully quipped at birth. Every child inherits certain characteristics from its ancestors. These are carried in the subconscious mind and brought into play when the life or health of the individual requires them.

It is natural to be born without pain, to develop without pain, to live without pain, and to die without pain. This is as natural as it is for a tree to blossom and bear fruit, which at the proper time drops off without distress. The subconscious will take care of every situation—even when it is interfered with it has a remedy available for every situation. Again, you forget something, but the subconscious mind has not forgotten; as soon as the conscious mind dismisses the matter, it comes to us.

Every engineer knows what it is to sleep over a problem. While he is asleep, the subconscious is working it out. Or he may lose an article, get excited and anxious about it, and not be able to find it;

but as soon as the conscious mind gives it up and lets go, the sense of where it is comes without effort.

Again, there is a difficult situation in your affairs, if you can only persuade your conscious mind to let go, to cease its anxiety, dismiss its fear, to give up the tenseness and struggle, then the subconscious will ordinarily bring about prosperity. The tendency of the subconscious is always toward health and harmonious conditions. To illustrate, you are in the water over your depth, you cannot swim, and you are sinking. If at the moment the life guard approaches you grab him around the neck and impede the actions of his arms and limbs, he mat be unable to do anything with you; but if you will simply trust yourself in his hands, then he will get you out. And so it is absolutely certain that the subconscious mind will be present in every difficult situation and that it will tend to play life guard in your favour—if you can but persuade your consciousness to cease its anxiety, to dismiss its fears, and to give up the tenseness of the struggle.

Suppose the conscious mind suffers itself to become angry over every trifle. Every time it gets angry, the impulse is transferred to the subconscious. The impulse is repeated again and again each time it is stirred up. The second record of anger is added to the first, the third to the second, and the forth to the third. Soon the subconscious has acquired the habit and before long it will be difficult to stop. When this situation develops, the conscious mind will be subject to the irritating influence from without and the habitual impulse from within. There will be action and reaction. It will be easier to be angry and more difficult to prevent it. Yet every time the conscious mind gets angry, an additional impulse will be given to the subconscious, and that impulse will be an additional incentive to get angry again.

Now then, anger is an abnormal condition, and any abnormal condition contains within itself the penalty, and this penalty will be promptly reflected in that part of the body that has the least resistance. For instance, if the person has a weak stomach, there will be acute attacks of indigestion, and eventually these will become chronic. In other persons, Bright's Disease[1] may develop; in another rheumatism; and so on.

---

1 Bright's Disease is a disease of the kidneys.

It is evident, therefore, that these conditions are effects; but if the cause be removed, the effects will vanish. If the individual knows that thoughts are causes and conditions are effects, he will promptly decide to control his thoughts. This will tend to erase anger and other bad mental habits; and as the light of truth gradually becomes clear and perfect, the habit and everything connected with it will be erased and the accumulated distress destroyed.

What is true of anger is true of jealousy, of fear, of lust, of greed, and of dishonesty—each of these may become subconscious and each of them may eventually result in some diseased condition of the body, and the nature of the disease indicates to the trained analyst the nature of the cause that was responsible for the condition.

Frederic Pierce tells us in *Our Unconscious Mind*:

"It is a matter of common observation that everyone is in greater or less degree suggestible. The reaction to suggestion may be either positive or negative, either an acceptance or heightened resistance. In this we see a censorship. An epidemic of a certain type of crime shows, on the part of the perpetrators, imitative response to suggestion implanted both by the elaborate descriptive accounts in the newspapers and by the great amount of discussion of the outrages heard on all sides.

"Primitive effects of great intensity are aroused; they break through the primary cultural censorship, which is weak in the criminally disposed person; they accumulate energy by being dwelt on in consciousness; and finally become sufficiently strong to surmount all fear of punishment and to control the conduct.

The remainder of the social group, having a higher cultural censorship, reacts to the same suggestion negatively and discharges the energy of whatever primitive effects have been aroused in the form of wrath and the desire for punishment of the criminals."

In this connection, it is interesting to note that one often hears the desire for vengeance expressed in terms of much greater primitive violence than the crime itself actually showed. Psycho-analysts hold that this is a method by which the individual is reinforcing his own none-too-strong censorship of his Unconscious.

PART TWENTY

METAPHYSICS

Creation consists in the art of combining forces that have an affinity for each other in the proper proportion. Thus, oxygen and hydrogen combined in the proper proportions produce water. Oxygen and hydrogen are both invisible gases, but water is not invisible.

Germs, however, have life; they must therefore be the product of something that has life or intelligence. Spirit is the only Creative Principle in the Universe, and Thought is the only activity that spirit possesses. Therefore, germs must be the result of a mental process.

A thought goes forth from the thinker; it meets other thoughts for which it has an affinity; they coalesce and form a nucleus for other similar thoughts; this nucleus sends out calls into the formless energy wherein all thoughts and all things are held in solution; and soon the thought is clothed in a form in accordance with the character given to it by the thinker.

A million men in the agony of death and torture on the battlefield send out thoughts of hatred and distress; soon another million men die form the effect of a microbe called "the influenza germ." None but the experienced metaphysician knows when and how the deadly germ came into existence.

As there are an infinite variety of thoughts, so there are an infinite variety of germs, constructive as well as destructive; but neither the constructive nor the destructive germ will germinate and flourish until it finds congenial soil in which to take root.

All thoughts and all things are held in solution in the Universal Mind. The individual may open his mental gates and thereby become receptive to thoughts of any kind or description. If he thinks that there are magicians, witches, or wizards who are desirous of injuring him, he is thereby opening the door for the entrance of such thoughts, and he will be able to say with Job, "The things I feared have come upon me." If, on the contrary, he thinks that there are those who are desirous of helping him, he thereby opens the door for such help, and he will find that "as thy faith is, so be it unto thee" is as true today as it was two thousand years ago.

Tolstoi[1] said: "Ever more and more clearly does the voice of reason become audible to man. Formerly men said: 'Do not think, but believe. Reason will deceive you; faith alone will open to you the true happiness of life.' And man tried to believe, but his relations with other people soon showed him that other men believed in something entirely different, so that soon it became inevitable that he must decide which faith out of many he would believe. Reason alone cannot decide this."

Attempts in our day to instill spiritual matters into man by faith, while ignoring his reason, are precisely the same as attempts to feed a man and ignore his mouth. Men's common nature has proven to them that they all have a common knowledge, and men will never more return to their former errors.

The voice of the people is the voice of God. It is impossible to drown that voice, because that voice is not the single voice of any one person, but the voice of all rational consciousness of mankind, which is expressed in every separate man.

Reason tells man that the Universe is a Cosmos and is therefore governed by law, so that when we see that some persons secure extraordinary results by mental or spiritual methods, reason tells us that we can all do exactly the same thing because the law is no respecter of persons, and that this is being done every day all the time, everywhere, is apparent to everyone who has taken the trouble to ascertain the facts.

All manifestations are governed by principles that we recognize as universal laws, and in the manifestation of those laws we recognize system, order, and harmony.

If the Infinite is omnipresent, it must encompass and interfiltrate all that seems to be matter and be one with it and inseparable from it.

Science teaches that so-called matter exists in a diversity of grades from its crudest visible form to the most refined and invisible state in an inseparable relationship with spirit, from which it can never be disassociated.

---

1 Lev Nikolayevich, Count Tolstoy (1828-1910) was a Russian author whose works include *War and Peace* and *Anna Karenina*.

The latent, or electric, power in the gaseous condition of the elements acts through vibration upon all matter in the combinations lower than the gases by induction, raising them also to a fluidic or gaseous condition and enabling them to form new combinations on a higher plane.

By the same principle is the mineral raised to the sphere of electricity, magnetism, or light, which of themselves are nothing more than ether in different velocities of vibration.

Radio activity consists in setting in motion certain electric vibrations, which after passing through the ether, record themselves on a distant receiver. The whole system depends on the intangible substance known as ether. It is a substance invisible, colorless, odorless, and inconceivably rarefied that fills all space. It fills the space between the earth and the sun and the stars, and it also fills the minute space between the atoms of the densest substance, such as steel. Even when electricity passes through a wire it is merely a vibration of the ether that circulates between the atoms composing the copper wire.

In turn, we have abundant proof of the subjugation of ethereal matter by the still more rarefied sphere of force that we recognize as *psychic force* or *mind force*.

Matter thus refined becomes the plastic associate of the mind for the transmission of it forces in the manifestation of its power.

That mind does transmit its forces through, or by, its vibrations, we have proof of the expression of its power of mind over mind, as in the manifestations of the mind of the hypnotist over his subject through mental suggestion, by which he is enabled to control the entire organism of his subject to such an extent as to suspend the functions of the organs of the body at will.

Thus we see that the subtle or refined elements of matter at the disposal of the mind are subject to his control. Matter in itself has no consciousness or feeling and is active only when controlled by spirit or mind in accordance with the laws that govern its action, and when active gives forth the manifestation and power of the spirit, mind, or intelligence behind it and acting upon it; and in its varied manifestations symbolizes the wisdom or intelligence of the mind of man or of the Infinite Mind itself.

As the infinite Mind rules and governs the Universe, so it is ordained for man to rule and govern his living Universe that he has created or evolved, known as "The Temple of the Living God," an abridgment or Microcosm of the Universe of the Infinite.

Wisdom is the proper use of knowledge to bring about harmony, happiness, ease, and health. Ignorance is the darkness that the light of truth disperses, which light alone can enable us to understand the priority of mind in the control of matter.

The office of metaphysics is to bring man into a true comprehension of his relationship with the world in which he lives, moves, and has his being, and an understanding of how to gain dominion over all that is his rightful heritage.

The metaphysician gives the patient nothing that he can see, nothing that he can hear, nothing that he can taste, nothing that he can smell, and nothing that he can feel. It is therefore absolutely impossible for the practitioner to reach the objective brain of the patient in any way whatsoever.

It will be said that he may give a mental suggestion—he may send him a thought. This might be possible if it were not for the fact that we do not consciously receive the thoughts of others except through the medium of the senses.

Again, admitting that it might be possible to reach the conscious mind without the aid of any material agency, the conscious or objective mind would not receive it because the objective mind is the mind with which we reason, plan, decide, will, and act. The practitioner invariably suggests perfection, and such a thought would be instantly dismissed by the objective mind as contrary to reason and therefore unacceptable, so that no result would be accomplished.

The Mind that the metaphysician calls into action is the Universal, not the individual. Their formula is: "Divine Mind always has met and always will meet every human need." This Divine Mind is the creative principle of the Universe. It is the "Father" that the Nazarene had in mind when he said:

> It is not I that doeth the work, but the Father that dwelleth within me. He doeth the work.

It will at once become apparent that this power that the metaphysician utilizes is spiritual, not material; subjective, not objective. For this reason it becomes necessary to reach the subconscious mind instead of the conscious mind. Here then is the secret of the efficacy of the method. The sympathetic nervous system is the organ of the subconscious mind. This system of nerves governs all of the vital processes of the body—the circulation of the blood, the digestion of the food, the building of tissues, the manufacture and distribution of the various secretions; in fact, the sympathetic nervous system reaches every part of the body. All vital processes are carried on subconsciously. They seem to have been purposely taken out of the realm of the conscious and placed under the control of a power that would be subject to no change or caprice.

The subjective mind, the subconscious mind, and the Divine Mind are therefore simply different terms of indicating the "One mind in which we live and move and have our being." We contact this mind by will or intention. Mind is Omnipresent—we may therefore contact it anywhere and everywhere, neither time nor space require consideration.

As spirit is the Creative Principle of the Universe, a subjective realization of this spiritual of man, and his consequent perfection, is taken up by the Divine Mind and eventually manifested in the life and experiences of the patient.

Some will say that this ideal state of perfection is never realized. To be sure, the Great Teacher anticipated this criticism, for did He not say: "In my Father's house are many mansions"?—indication that there are many degrees of perfection; that although the law operates with immutable precision, the operator may be uninformed or inexperienced. The ability to throw the thought up and beyond the evidence of the senses into the realm of the uncreated, where all that ever was of ever will be is waiting to be brought forth, to be organized, developed, and crystallized into tangible form, is not the work of the enthusiast who has just come into the knowledge of his spiritual inheritance. It is rather the work of one who has become responsive to the most subtle vibrations, he who can hear the Voice of the Silence, he who has come into the terrible realization that the oasis he saw as he passed over the desert was but a mirage, and as he approached, it receded; he who is no longer astonished or amazed to find that after all, real power is impersonal, that it may make a super-beast of one and a super-man of another.

A great many do not understand the Principle of Metaphysics and the method of applying it so as to work intelligently in their own behalf. Under such conditions, they can only expect to rely on some one else, and when that is done continually or at frequent intervals, it tends to weaken rather than strengthen the spiritual factor in consciousness.

It is, therefore, desirable and necessary to secure an understanding of the nature of Truth. Most persons who have become interested in Metaphysics have had some wonderful experience or they know of some one who has had such an experience.

It has been declared by philosophers, religionists, and scientists, again and again, that no proof of the existence of the absolute Truth is possible. In other words, that the only way in which a man can be convinced of the creative power of Truth is by demonstration, or by assuming that Truth is all powerful and then on the basis of this assumption make the demonstration. This is *proof*, this is freedom, this is why it is has been said: "Ye shall know the truth and the truth shall make you free."

Observation of the characteristic manifestations of anything and deductions based upon such observation constitute knowledge of that thing; it will readily be seen, therefore, that if you have observed and have become aware of the fact of certain characteristic manifestations of Truth, you will have knowledge. If it should come to pass that you had observed and carefully noted *all* the characteristic manifestations of Truth, and then in addition perceived the uniformities that run through those manifestations, especially if they are complex, and see the laws or system upon which their characteristics are based, then your knowledge of Truth would be complete.

Through the mental and spiritual awakening of a century ago, which was responsible for modern progressive thought, certain higher forces and principles were discovered in the mind of man; and in the same way new realms of thought and spiritual reality were opened to consciousness—revelations, literally, that gave life a changed and marvelous meaning and that caused the cosmos to extend into infinity, seemingly, in every direction. And therefore a twofold purpose appeared at the very beginning of this movement—to know the Real Man and to know the Real Cosmos. An ancient desire, but which was reborn at this time, and with so much virility that it has become today a soulful passion in the minds of millions.

What, then, are the characteristics of Truth? All agree that in the philosophical sense Truth is that which is absolute and changeless. Truth must then be a fact. What then is a fact? Well, three times three equals nine. That is a fact—always was a fact, always will be a fact; there can be no evasion, no argument, no equivocation. It is truth in the United States, in China, in Japan; it is true everywhere; all the time. A fact exists in the nature of things without beginning, without end, without limitation. It governs out actions and our commercial operations. Those who would undertake to disregard it would do so at their peril. It is, however, a fact which you cannot see, you cannot hear, you cannot taste, nor can you smell or feel it—it is not apprehensible to any of the physical senses. Is it therefore any less a fact? It is without color, size, or form; is it for this reason any less true? It is without years; is it for that reason not the same yesterday, today, and forever?

You may use this fact as long as you live. Millions of other persons may use it as often as they like. That will not destroy it. Use does not change it; from everlasting to everlasting—three times three equals nine. This is therefore a fact or the Truth.

Truth is the only possible knowledge that man can possess, because knowledge that is not based upon truth would be false and would therefore not be knowledge at all.

Counterfeit money is not true money. It is false, however much it may pass for true. The Truth is, therefore, all that any one can know, for what is not true does not exist, therefore we cannot know it. We all think we know much that is not so, but what is not so does not exist, therefore we cannot know it.

Therefore, the Truth or absolute knowledge is the only possible knowledge and any other use of the word is not scientific or exact.

The metaphysicians of the East will not give out spiritual knowledge miscellaneously. They will not give it to children or young people except under conditions when they have them directly under control and directly under instruction as definitely as we have our children under instruction in the intellectual life in our schools.

In India, when a young man is to be initiated into things spiritual, a definite seven years course is provided for him under a master, and he is given first the things that he first ought to know along these lines. He is forewarned with regard to dangers that may arise and the whole course of his journey is guarded by his master with the greatest care, so as to prevent his stumbling during the early stages.

If spiritual metaphysics becomes popular in our Western world, the same things will develop here. People will not take up the most advanced work before becoming acquainted with the simpler forms of knowledge. Attainment implies obligation: If you are somewhere up the ladder of culture, if you have entered the school of understanding, if you have seen the light of spiritual Truth, then you are supposed by that very fact to know more than the one who has not yet arrived. Your nervous system will automatically organize itself on a higher plane, and because of this you must live closer to the law of your being or experience suffering more quickly. There are no exceptions to the law.

The resurrection from the dead is not a process of getting corpses out of the grave. It is the elevation of mentalities from the plane of the material to the plane of the spiritual. It is crossing the river Jordan and entering the "Promised Land." It is not until one becomes acquainted with the laws governing in the spiritual world that he really begins to "live." Consequently, those who are still functioning in the material world are "dead"—they have not yet been resurrected. "Eyes have they but they see not, ears have they but they hear not."

Those who have been raised to the spiritual plane find that there are many practices that they must drop. In most cases, these practices leave the individual without difficulty. They drop away of their own accord. But when the individual persists in functioning in the old world, he usual find that "A house divided against itself cannot stand,"[1] and he frequently must suffer severely before he learns that he cannot violate spiritual laws with impunity.

---

1 Matthew 12:25. "And Jesus knew their thoughts, and said unto them, Every kingdom divided against itself is brought to desolation; and every city or house divided against itself shall not stand."

Mind in itself is believed to be a subtle form of static energy, from which arises the activities called "thought," which is the dynamic phase of mind. Mind is static energy, thought is dynamic energy—the two phases of the same thing.

—**Walker**

PART TWENTY-ONE

PHILOSOPHY

Silence

In silence was the Universe conceived,
In silence doth the heart of man seek out
That other heart to rest on; Nature's soul
Yearns ceaselessly to give its speechless calm
Unto her restless children as they roam
Far from that central place which is their home.

Wouldst know thy Mother Nature face to face?
Wouldst hear her silent heartbeats? Close thine ears
And still thy senses; wouldst thou feel her arms
Enfold thy being? Thou must give thyself
In uttermost abandon to her will
That she may teach thee the one truth—be still!

Be still—and from the Silence shall arise
A mem'ry of forgotten mysteries.
A healing peace descending on thy soul
Shall bear it up to regions beyond words
Where thou shalt learn the secrets of the earth,
Of wind and flame and how the stars have birth.

Then shalt thou know thy heritage of joy;
Borne on the pinions of the Bird of Life,
Tuned to the rhythm of revolving spheres,
Feeling with all that breathes, with all that strives
For union with its prototype above,
The silent comforter whose name is—Love.

—Frances Poile

Physical science has resolved matter into molecules, molecules into atoms, atoms into energy, and it has remained for Mr. J.A. Fleming[1], in an address before the Royal Institution, to resolve this energy into mind. He says:

> In its ultimate essence, energy may be incomprehensible by us except as an exhibition of the direct operation of that which we call Mind or Will.

We find, therefore, that science and religion are not in conflict, but are in perfect agreement. Mr. Leland[2] makes this quite plain. In an article on "World Making" he says:

"First, there is wisdom that has planned, and so adjusted, all the parts of the universe in such a perfect balance that there is no friction. And as the universe is infinite, the wisdom that has planned it must be infinite, too.

"Secondly, there is a will that has fixed and ordained the activities and forces of the universe and bound them by laws inflexible and eternal. And everywhere this Omnipotent Will has established the limitations and directions of the energies and processes, and has fixed their everlasting stability and uniformity.

"And as the universe is Infinite, this Will must be Infinite.

"And thirdly, there is a power that sustains and moves, a power that never wearies, a power which controls all forces; and, as the universe in Infinite, the Power must be Infinite, too. What shall we name this Infinite trinity—Wisdom, Will, and Power? Science knows no simpler name for it than God. This name is all embracing."

We can conceive of something of its meaning, though we cannot comprehend its significance. And this Being is the indwelling and ultimate. He is imminent in matter as in spirit; and to Him all Law, Life, Force, must be referred. He is the sustaining, energizing, all-pervading Spirit of the universe.

Every living thing must be sustained by this Omnipotent Intel-

1 Sir John Ambrose Fleming (1849-1945) was an English engineer who made various contributions to electronics.
2 Samuel Phelps Leland (1839-1910) was an American poet and author.

ligence, and we find the difference in individual lives to be largely measured by the degree of this intelligence that they manifest. It is a greater intelligence that places the animal in a higher scale of being than the plant, the man higher than the animal; and we find this increased intelligence is again indicated by the power of the individual to control modes of action and thus to consciously adjust himself to his environment. It is this adjustment that occupies the attention of the greatest minds and this adjustment consists in nothing else than the recognition of an existing order in the Universal Mind, for it is well known that this mind will obey us precisely in proportion as we first obey it.

As we increase in experience and development, there is a corresponding increase in the exercise of the intellect, in the range and power of feeling, in the ability to choose, in the power to will, in all executive action, in all self-consciousness. That would mean that self-consciousness is increasing, expanding, growing, developing, and enlarging. It increases and develops because it is a spiritual activity; we multiply our possession of spiritual things in proportion to our use of them. All material things are consumed in the using. There is a diametrically opposite law governing the use of the spiritual and the material.

Life is that quality or principle of the Universal energy that manifests in so-called organic objects as growth and voluntary activity, and which is usually co-existent in some degree with some manifestation of that same Universal Energy as the quality or principle termed intelligence. There is only one Supreme Principle evading all comprehension of its essential nature. It is the Absolute. Man can think only in terms of the relative. Therefore, he sometimes defines it as the Universal Intelligence, the Universal Substance, as Ether, Life, mind, Spirit, Energy, Truth, Love, etc. His particular definition at any moment is governed by the particular relationship of the phenomena of Being in which he thinks of this Principle at that moment.

Mind is present in the lowest forms of life, in the protoplasm, or cell. The protoplasm, or cell, perceives its environment, initiates motion, and chooses its food. All these are evidences of mind. As an organism develops and becomes more complex, the cells begin to specialize, some doing one thing and some another, but all of them showing intelligence. By association their mind powers increase.

Whereas in the beginning, each function of life and each action is the result of conscious thought, the habitual actions become automatic or subconscious in order that the self-conscious mind may attend to other things. The new actions will, however, in their turn, become habitual, then automatic, then subconscious, in order that the mind again may be freed from this detail and advance to still other activities.

Until very recently, it was said that matter, in its ultimate nature, was eternal; though all the forms thereof change. We were told that a building destroyed by fire with nothing but a few ashes left had gone up in smoke and gas and that only the form of the manifestation had changed; that the essential substances were still in existence in different chemical formations.

We were told that all forms of matter exist in the form of molecules; that these molecules are resolvable into certain smaller elements called atoms. Until recently, the atom was supposed to be the ultimate particle of matter, so until recently scientists supposed that matter could be resolved into atoms and that was final.

But with the discovery of radium, it was found that the atom is made up if a large number of smaller particles called electrons or ions, and these electrons vary according to the kind of atom that is under consideration. A hydrogen atom contains a different number of electrons than an oxygen atom, and so on.

The atoms within the molecules are separated from each other by very great distances as compared with their diameter. The electrons in turn are separated from each other by distances as compared to the diameter as are the planets in the solar system. When we remember that the molecule, which is the larger of the group, is so small that it cannot be discovered by the most powerful microscope, so small that you could place many millions of them into an ordinary thimble, you can conceive how infinitesimal is the ultimate particle of matter called the electron or ion.

It has been discovered that the atoms of radium are constantly radiating their ions into space, producing what is called radioactivity; that these particles are apparently lost, they simply vanish.

Finally, it has been discovered that other forms of matter besides radium are throwing off their ions into space, and that these seem to be absolutely lost in the process. Thus, the atoms of matter are constantly wasting away so that the modern physicist no longer claims that matter is indestructible. It is in a constant state of flux—it is forever changing in form.

What then is the director which controls the action of the ion, which indicates the form that it is to take? Mind is the director and this direction is the process called creation.

It will therefore readily be seen that the basis upon which matter rests is mind or spirit. The spirit of a thing is, therefore, the thing itself. It is the spirit of a thing that attracts to itself the necessary electrons for its development from the ether and which are gradually assembled by the law of growth. It is evident, therefore, that the saying of Saint Paul is true:

"The things which are seem are temporal, but the things which are not seen are eternal."

Many years ago, John Bovee Dods[1] wrote:

> We have mounted from lead up to electricity, and though as we rose, we found each successive substance more easily moved than the one below it, still we have not as yet found a single material that possesses inherent motion as its attribute. Lead, rock, earth, and water are moved by impulse. Air is moved by rarefaction and electricity is moved by the positive and negative forces. True we have mounted up, as before remarked, to electricity; but even this cannot move unless it is thrown out of balance in relation to quantity as to its positive and negative forces.
>
> Electricity is a fluid most inconceivably subtle, rarefied, and fine. It is computed to require four mil-

1 John Bovee Dods (1795-1872) was a philosopher born in New York City. His life was devoted to mental philosophy.

lion particles of our air to make a speck as large as the smallest visible grain of sand, and yet electricity is more than seven hundred thousand times finer than air! It is almost unparticled matter, and is not only invisible, but so far as we can judge, it is imponderable.

It cannot be seen—it cannot be weighed! A thousand empty Leyden jars, capable of containing a gallon each, may be placed upon the nicest scale and most accurately weighed. Then let these be filled with electricity and, so far as human sagacity can determine, they will weigh no more. Hence to our perception a thousand gallons weigh nothing.

As electricity in regard to motion stands upon the poise being completely balanced by the positive and negative forces that equalize each other, so it is easily perceived that if we mount one step higher, we must come to that substance whose nature is to move, and the result of that motion is thought and power. It is ***mind***. Hence, it will be distinctly perceived, in view of the argument now offered, that we cannot, as philosophers, stop short of motion in the highest and most sublime substance in being. This conclusion is absolutely and positively irresistible, and challenges refutation.

When we mount up in our contemplations through the various grades of matter and see it continually brightening—as we press onward in our delightful career of rapture until we arrive at that sublimed substance which can be neither seen nor weighed, which moves with a velocity of twelve million miles per minute and can travel around this globe in the eighth part of a second—we are struck with astonishment and awe! But as this is not the last link in the immeasurable chain, we are forced to proceed onward until we arrive at the finest, most sublime, and brilliant substance in being—a substance that possesses the attributes of inherent or self-motion and living power, and from which all other motion and power throughout the immeasurable universe are derived. This is the Infinite Mind, and possesses embodied form. It is a living being. This Infinite Mind comes in contact with electricity, gives to it motion, arms it with power, and through this almighty unseen agent, moves the universe and carries on all the multifarious operations of nature.

Hence, there is not a motion that transpires amidst the immensity of His works, from rolling globes to the falling leaf, but what originates in the Eternal Mind, and by Him is performed, through electricity as His agent. Mind is, therefore, the absolute perfection of all substances in being; and as it possesses self-motion as its grand attribute, so it is, in this respect, exactly the reverse of all other substances, which are, of themselves, motionless. Mind, or spirit, is above all, and absolutely disposes and controls all. Hence, Mind is imponderable, invisible, and eternal.

PART TWENTY-TWO

SCIENCE

The Thinker

Back of the beating hammer,
By which the steel is wrought,
Back of the workshop's clamor,
The seeker may find the Thought;
The thought that is ever master
Of iron and steam and steel,
That rises above disaster
And tramples it under heel!

—Berton Braley

Science is not idealistic, nor spiritualistic, nor materialistic, but simply natural; she seeks to learn everywhere facts and their logical corollaries, without doing homage in advance to a system in this or in that direction. "Science," says Grove[1], "should have neither desires nor prejudices; truth should be her sole aim."

Huxley[2] says, "Modern science has made its way into the works of our best poets, and even the man of letters is unconsciously impregnated with her spirit and indebted for his best products to her methods. I believe that the greatest intellectual revolution mankind has yet seen is now slowly taking place by her agency. She is teaching the world that the ultimate course of appeal is observation and experiment, and not authority; she is teaching it to estimate the value of evidence; she is creating a firm and living faith in the existence of immutable moral and physical laws, perfect obedience to which is the highest possible aim of an intelligent being."

Redi[3] did not trouble himself much with speculative consideration, but attacked particular cases of what was supposed to be "spontaneous generation" experimentally.

"Here are dead animals, or pieces of meat," he says. "I expose them to the air in hot weather and in a few days they swarm with maggots. You tell me these are generated in the dead flesh; but if I put similar bodies, while quite fresh, in a jar and tie some fine gauze over the top of the jar, not a maggot makes its appearance, while the dead substances, nevertheless, putrefy in the same way as before. It is obvious, therefore, that the maggots are not generated by the corruption of the meat and that the cause of their formation must be something which is kept away by gauze. But gauze will not keep away aeriform bodies or fluids. This something must, therefore, exist in the form of solid particles too big to get through the gauze. Nor is one long left in doubt what these solid particles are; for the bow-flies, attracted by the odor of the meat, swarm round the vessel and, urged by powerful but in each case mislead-

1 Sir William Robert Grove (1811-1896) was a scientist who is 1839 developed the first fuel cell.

2 Thomas Henry Huxley (1825-1895) was an English biologist who was a staunch defender of Darwin.

3 Francesco Redi (1626-1697) was an Italian physician whose experiments disproved abiogenisis, or the spontaneous generation of life.

ing instinct, lay eggs out of which the maggots are immediately hatched upon the gauze. The conclusion, therefore, is unavoidable: the maggots are not generated by the meat, but the eggs which give rise to them are brought through the air by the flies."

These experiments seem almost childishly simple and one wonders how it was that no one ever thought of them before. Simple as they are, however, they are worthy of the most careful study, for every piece of experimental work done in regard to this subject has been shaped upon the model furnished by the Italian philosopher. As the results of his experiments were the same, however varied the nature of the materials he used, it is not wonderful that there arises in Redi's mind a presumption that, in all such cases of the seeming production of life from dead matter, the real explanation was the introduction of living germs from without into that dead matter. And thus the hypothesis that living matter always arises by the agency of pre-existing living matter took definite shape; and had, henceforward, a right to be considered and a claim to be refuted, in each particular case, before the production of living matter in any other way could be admitted by careful reasoners.

That which endures is not one or another association of living forms, but the process of which the cosmos is the product, and of which these are among the transitory expressions. And in the living world, one of the most characteristic features of this cosmic process is the struggle for existence, the competition of each with all, the result of which is the selection, that is to say, the survival of those forms which, on the whole, are best adapted to the conditions that at any period obtain; and which are therefore, in that respect (and only in that respect) the fittest. The acme reached by the cosmic process in the vegetation of the downs is seen in the turf, with its weeds and gorse. Under the conditions, they have come out of the struggle victorious; and, by surviving, have proved that they are the fittest to survive.

In the life of the mind, there must eventually be some features of absolute unity, despite the diversity that may exist in its organization. The laws of thinking are no doubt the same throughout the universe.

Just as it is possible to show in the physical development of the organ of thought an uninterrupted scale of gradual development from the lowest animal to the highest human being, so a similar ascent of psychical and mental properties in every rising development may be found in him. Neither morphology, nor chemistry, nor macroscopy, nor microscopy is capable of discovering an essential difference between human and animal brains. Great though the differences may be, they are after all but differences of degree. This accounts for the absolute failure that has attended all the attempts made by some scientists, even down to our own time, to discover any such characteristic or essential differences, and on the strength of these to assign to man a special place and classification in natural history.

Prof. William McDougall[1], the distinguished professor of psychology at Harvard, in a session of the British Association for the Advancement Science at Toronto, made this very significant announcement.

"Thirty to forty years ago, when I began to study science, considerable moral courage would have been required to insist upon the purposive nature of man. For at that time the great wave of scientific materialism was still but little past its climax. It was the day of Spencer and Huxley, of Clifford and Tyndal, of Lange and Weismann, of Verworm and Bain. The world and all the living things in it were presented to us with so much prestige and confidence, as one vast system of mechanistic determination that one seemed to be placed before two acutely opposed alternatives.

"On the one hand, science and universal mechanism; on the other hand, humanism, religion, mysticism, and superstition.

"But the physical universe of eternal hard atoms and universal elastic ether, the realm of pure mechanics, has become a welter of entities and activities which change in development and disappear like the figures of the kaleidoscope. The atoms are gone; matter has resolved itself into energy; and what energy is no man can tell, beyond saying it is the possibility of change, of further evolution.

"In psychology, the mechanistic confidence of the nineteenth

1 William McDougall (1871-1938) was a psychologist whose work greatly influenced the theory of instinct and social psychology.

century is fading away as the complexity of the living organism is more fully realized, as its powers of compensation, self-regulation, reproduction, and repair are more fully explored.

"In general biology, the mechanistic neo-Darwinism is bankrupt before the problems of evolution, the origin of variation and mutations, the predominance of mind in the later stages of the evolutionary process, the indications of purposive striving at even the lowest levels, the combination of marvelous persistency of type with indefinite plasticity which pervades the realm of life and which finds its only analog in the steadfast purposive adaptive striving of a resolute personality."

Sir Oliver Lodge[1] says, among scientific men the ether has only been studied by physicists, and not by all of them. It has been ignored by chemists and has probably never entered the thought of physiologists or biologists of any kind at all. And yet, if it is a reality in the universe, it may have chemical and biological functions to perform, as well as its well-known functions in the science of physics. We know it familiarly in the phenomena of light, of electricity, of magnetism. We are beginning to associate it also, rather definitely, with elasticity, cohesion, and gravitation. And we are gradually learning that the greater part of the energy in the universe (and certainly all potential energy) belongs to it, and not to matter at all. Atomic matter is one thing; the ether is another. They may be related. The link between them is electricity. But if it is possible ever to unify them and to regard them as different manifestations of one thing, there is no doubt which is the more fundamental of the two. The ether is the fundamental thing. Matter is a derived and secondary thing. And the electric charges which constitute matter are probably composed of modifications of the ether.

And it is because they lack the clue that biologists in general feel so hostile and are conscious of such repugnance to the facts themselves. To the honour of Professor Richet[2], in spite of his re-

---

1 Sir Oliver Joseph Lodge (1851-1940) was a physicist involved in the development of the wireless telegraph.

2 Charles Robert Richet (1850-1935) was a French physiologist who won the Nobel Prize for Medicine in 1913 for his work on anaphlaxis, a condition where a patient would sometimes die from a second injection of an antigen.

pugnance, he is ready to accept the facts. But it seems to me that he raises unnecessary difficulties about them by his insistence on matter alone. He will never understand them in terms of "matter" alone. Strictly speaking, we cannot understand anything fully and completely in terms of matter alone. By concentrating on matter, we eliminate from our thoughts the greater part of the universe. The universe contains many things besides matter. It contains magnetism and electricity and light and ether; it also contains life and thought and mind and consciousness and memory and personality and character. None of these things are material, and yet, strangely enough, some of them have come into association with matter through the curious biological process of incarnation.

Albert Edward Wiggam[1] says,

"And now, today, in the electron of the atom and in the germ cell of living protoplasm, we have at last come upon God in His own workshop. The mechanist has looked about this workshop and exclaimed, 'It is all machinery.' The spiritualist has said, 'Behind it is the breath of God.' One has found a universe that works; the other a universe that is significant. One has found the tools; the other the workman. But whether he be mechanist or vitalist, materialist or spiritualist, both are agreed that cooperation with natural law—the will of God—is the only righteousness. This alone is organic morality. This alone is progress."

I do not know what philosophy is true. I only know that unfettered philosophic thought is the only thing that can lead us to the things that are true. And I am pleading for the importance and influence of truth and that it may be in our time bravely lifted up for all men.

However, if I am to trust my extremely diffident interpretation of Prof. John Dewey[2], science and the critical speculation that has come into the world with have given two great new trends to philosophy; all of which, I think, are of great importance to the statecraft.

1 Albert Edward Wiggam (1871 - 1957) was an American biologist who became famous for his quotes about knowledge and education.
2 John Dewey (1859-1952) was an American philosopher and educational reformer who argued that education should have practical applications and not just be an abstract tool.

First, philosophy has changed as to its theory of knowledge—the very nature of the knowing processes of the mind. Biology has made this contribution. From the old notion that knowledge was built up out of independent sensations, that is, that the senses were the gateways to knowledge, biology has contributed the new conception that knowledge is behavior, the reaction, the "hitting back" of a living organism upon its environment. Knowledge thus becomes the active, operative experience of an organism carrying out the rich possibilities of the inherent structure. Not to go into technical jargon, all the old psychology that underlaid both the rationalism of the rationalist and the empiricism of the empiricist is thus completely exploded so that we can hardly realize what has become of it.

Second, this change as to the nature of knowledge has brought enormous changes in our conceptions as to the nature of truth, as to what truth is and what is true. We find that truth and the way we gain knowledge are quite bound together. The old notion of a realm of unchangeable truth out in the sky somewhere has become transformed into a conception of truth as a working, living thing. Thus, the old battle between the real and the ideal, subject and object, experience and reason, noumenon and phenomenon, have become strangely obsolete because they are seen to have no practical consequence.

For society is suffering primarily not from unbalanced budgets and disrupted ententes, but from wrong mental processes. Many of these processes have become institutions; for institutions, as Martin says, are simply stereotyped social habits. Consequently, the way men think is the thing that makes right or wrong, wise or foolish institutions. And there are great wrong mental processes—some of them age-old institutions—that prevent the inner life from expanding to meet the new needs, and prevent them from breathing the spacious airs of a new spiritual morning with which science is ready to light the world. These mental habits are not called evils because they lie so far behind our obvious evils that they are not discerned. They do not make good newspaper headlines. Juries and investigating committees never list them as the "causes" of social breakdown because the juries and committees are themselves caught up in the same network of habit. But until they are observed and corrected, society can never become intelligent. And until society becomes intelligent, it can never become happy or free.

In *An Unorthodox Conception of Being*, William Ellsworth Hermance says: "We are forced to view matter as of two planes: the material and the spiritual. The single atom is not material, it is spiritual; that is, it is simply a definite amount of Power, and the Power alone would be absolutely immaterial."

Premising that the atoms are conscious is totally different from stating that the material is conscious. The inorganic atoms (the atoms unorganized) are not conscious on the material plane.

One of the errors of Materialism is in assuming that matter under certain forms may be conscious, as in the brain. They assume that as we are conscious, it must be some material portion of the person that is conscious. There is absolutely no proof that consciousness is created either as a result of motion or form, which is the Monistic idea; or that it is a physical product due to a peculiar combination of matter, which is the idea of some Materialists.

Is it illogical or unreasonable to say the motion must primarily be carried back to the molecule and the atom? If it is so carried, the atom or the individual is where the consciousness lies.

It takes more to constitute what we mean by an army than even all the persons which compose the army. The personal constituents of a mob might be exactly the same as those of the army. The difference is that one is organized and the other is not.

My hypothesis is that the Universal Power is conscious and intelligent; that each part is conscious and intelligent, but as parts cannot be equal to the whole, so no atom or ego is equal in intelligence to the whole. On the other hand, I believe the whole is no greater than all of its parts collectively and organically, and each part is as essential to the whole, proportionally, as the whole is to the part.

I do not conceive of any density whatever of the atoms. Density is an attribute of the material and one atom in not material, it is spirit, and has no material attributes. This is a typical point of difference between my conception and the materialistic conception. If the atom of hydrogen does not penetrate the parchment as readily as the atom of oxygen does, why? Unless the oxygen atom is smaller, why does it penetrate better?

There is, therefore, in the living organism something besides mere physical forces or the chemistry of dead nature—something that ceases to be when life ceases. There is a vital condition in which molecules have powers that lead to resulting seed-bearing structures widely different from those of inorganic nature, and standing on altogether a higher level. There is a power of evolution, an architectural power, that not only exalts chemical results, but evolves a diversity of parts and structures and a heritage of ancestral qualities of which the laws of material mature give no explanation.

August Comte[1] says that "the positive spirit consists in keeping oneself equally distant from two dangers—mysticism and empiricism." By mysticism he understands the recourse to non-verifiable explanations and to transcendent hypotheses. Men's imagination finds pleasure in these things, but we must be able to bring all "real" knowledge back to a general or particular fact. Positive science, therefore, abstains from searching after substances, ends, and even causes. It only bears upon phenomena and their relations.

When, by means of observation or deduction, he has arrived at a knowledge of their laws, he remains satisfied. For the knowledge of these laws allows him in certain cases to intervene in the phenomena and to substitute to the natural order an artificial order better suited to his requirements. It is thus that mechanical, astronomical, physical, chemical, and even biological phenomena are objects of relative and positive science for him today.

But, as soon as the question is one of facts which originate in the human conscience or which are connected with social life and with history, as opposite tendency becomes predominant. Instead of solely seeking for the laws of phenomena, our mind desires to explain them. It want to find the essence and the cause.

The confused disturbing movements which fill the world with

---

1 Auguste Comte (1798-1857) was a French philosopher and the "father" of sociology. He was the founder of Positivism, which is the system of thought that maintains that the goal of knowledge is to merely describe the phenomena rather than to debate its existence.

trouble and agitation and which, unless rational harmony be at last established threaten it destruction, are not due merely to political causes. They proceed from moral disorder. And this in turn proceeds from intellectual disorder; that is to say, from a lack of principles common to call minds and from the absence of universally admitted conceptions and beliefs. For in order that a human society may subsist, a certain harmony of sentiment or even common interests among its members will not suffice. Above all things, intellectual concord that finds expression in a body of common beliefs is necessary.

The number of men with sufficient leisure and enough culture to examine these conclusions and to go into their proofs will always be small. The attitude of the others must be one of submission and respect. But, differing on this point from the religious dogmas that humanity has known until now, the new faith will be "demonstrated." It will contain nothing that has not been established and controlled by scientific methods, nothing that goes beyond the domain of the relative, nothing that at any moment cannot be proved to a mind capable of following the demonstration.

This form of "faith" already exists in the case of a great number of scientific truths. Thus, all men today believe in the theory of the solar system that we owe to Copernicus, to Galileo, and to Newton. Yet how many are in a position to understand the demonstrations upon which this theory rests? They know, however, that what here is a matter of faith to them, is a matter of science to others, and would be so equally for themselves had they gone through the necessary studies.

The faith that is born of knowledge finds its object in an eternal order, bringing forth ceaseless change, through endless time, in endless space; the manifestation of the cosmic energy alternating between phases of potentiality and phases of explication.

The Deity and the Universe are but one substance, at the same time both spirit and matter, thought and extension, which are the only known attributes of the Deity.

And if, as there is not the least reason to doubt, more highly organized living begins to exist in remote worlds, these would yet, in their superior development as rational beings, undoubtedly resemble the earth-man in regard to intellect, since in the whole universe only one intelligence can be imagined that is the same everywhere—an intelligence that makes all physical laws appear as intellectual laws.

Alexander Thomas Ormand, professor of philosophy, Princeton University, says:

"There is a kind of popular knowledge that is not science, and this has its own value as the plain man's case goes to show, but this species soon reaches its limit, and, as a whole, it is found to be unreliable except for the roughest kind of approximation. There is, then, a threatened breakdown of the whole business of experience which is only averted by the rise of science and its exact methods. Whatever may have been true of the ancients, it is certainly the case that modern life would have been impossible without the aid of science. This help is has not been merely practical. Modern science has given us a new heaven and a new earth. It has enlarged our conceptions, revolutionized our methods, and immeasurably extended the scope of our ideas of reality. It is not too much to say that the world in which we moderns live, if it had been dreamed by an ancient, would have been regarded as too extravagant for even the kind of credence that was then attached to dreams.

"The truth is, when we begin to apprehend the vast function modern science has performed in the drama of modern experience, the danger is not that science will not obtain due recognition, but that it will claim a monopoly. This tendency can be redressed only by combining with a generous recognition of the place which science holds in the philosophical synthesis, an insight into the fact that there is another point of view from which consciousness becomes primate and leads to the concepts and methods of another discipline. The philosophical synthesis begins with science, but it reaches its conclusion in metaphysics.

"Suppose that we have grounds for asserting the existence of an absolute in the world. Have we any resources in our experience that will enable us to render this absolute in any sense intelligible?

"It will be clear that the reality if the idea of God will be measured by its ability to harmonize with, and in a true sense to unify, all the other real interests and ideals in life. We are in a bad predicament when our culture points east, our science north, and our religion south. To one the elements of whose experience are in such chaos as this, the idea of God cannot, in the nature of the case, have much significance. But let us suppose that our culture and our science are at one in the line of truth and that our political ideals all center in the line of good. If, then, our idea of God be that of a being in whose experience the true and the good are unified so that there can be no conflict, our religion then becomes the principle that unifies all the elements of our life and the idea of God becomes the central force in our experience. Now it is clear that the normal function of such an idea as that of God is one of unification. God stands as the ideally complete realization of all we may aspire to. He is simply the soul writ, not in large, but in transcendent terms, and the idea of Him is one that ideally comprehends and completes all the elements of our experience. Naturally, then, the idea of God ought to bear to our experience and all its elements the relation of a unifying principle. The reality of the idea of God depends, therefore, on the degree to which it vitally relates itself to our experience. Were it a mere abstraction without any close connection with the life of man it could lay little claim to reality. But that has the highest claim to reality which not only touches experience vitally at every point, but is also necessary to it as its ideal and its unifying principle."

We find, therefore, in the statements of many of the greatest living scientists that pure science and pure religion are in absolute harmony, and Prof. J.S. Haldane[1], the eminent British scientist, goes on to say:

"It is only when science is dogmatic that it assumes an attitude which seems to deny the existence of spiritual reality. But, there is very little of this dogmatism in the writings of the great men of science though very much in the desiccated science of text books and popular expositions."

---

1 John Burdon Sanderson Haldane (1892-1964) was a British geneticist and evolutionary biologist.

'Tis not in Time but in man's thought
That aught of good or ill is wrought;
His word is law, his thought is fate,
Time is his servant and must wait.
To bring whate'er he may decree,
Each mortal holds "The Master-Key,"
O'er Time and Fate and Destiny.

—Henry Victor Morgan

PART TWENTY-THREE

RELIGION

Look to This Day.
For it is Life, the very Life of Life.
In Its brief course lie all the Verities and
Realities of your existence;
The Bliss of Growth;
The Glory of Action;
The Splendor of Beauty;
For Yesterday is but a Dream,
And Tomorrow is only a Vision;
But Today well lived makes every
Yesterday a Dream of Happiness, and
Every Tomorrow a Vision of Hope.
Look well, therefore, to This Day!

—From the Sanskrit

Destiny is determined, for nations and for individuals, by factors and forces that are really fundamental—such as men's attitude toward one another. Ideals and motives are more potent than events in shaping History. What people think about the abiding concerns of life means more than any contemporary agitation or upheaval.

A few centuries ago it was thought that we must choose between the Bible and Galileo. Fifty years ago it was thought that we must choose between the Bible and Darwin, but as Dean W. R. Inge[1], of St. Paul's Cathedral, London, says:

> Every educated man knows that the main facts of organic evolution are firmly established, and that they are quite different from the legends borrowed by the ancient Hebrews from the Babylonians. We are not required to do violence to our reason by rejecting the assured results of modern research. Traditional Christianity must be simplified and spiritualized. It is at present encumbered by bad science and caricatured by bad economics and the more convinced we are of this, the less disposed we shall be to stake the existence of our faith on superstitions which are the religion of the irreligious and the science of the unscientific.

Modern discontent and unsatisfactory conditions are the symptoms of a deep seated and destructive disease. Remedies applied to these symptoms in the form of legislation and suppression may relieve the symptoms, but they do not cure the disease that will manifest in other and worse symptoms. Patches applied to an old decaying and obsolete garment in no way improve the garment. Constructive measures must be applied to the foundations of our civilization and that is our thought.

A philosophy of life having as its basis blind optimism, a religion that won't work seven days a week or a proposition that isn't

---

1 William Ralph Inge (1860-1954) was an English author and professor of divinity at Cambridge. He was also a columnist for the *Evening Standard.*

practical appeals to the intelligent not at all. It is results that we want and to all such the acid test is: Will it work?

The apparent impossibilities are the very things that help us to realize the possible. We must go over the unbeaten trail of thought, cross the desert of ignorance, wade through the "Swamp of Superstition," and scale the mountains of rites and ceremonies if we ever expect to come into the "promised land of revelation." Intelligence rules! Thought intelligently directed is a creative force that automatically causes its object to manifest on a material plane. *Let him that hath an ear to hear, hear!*

One of the characteristic signs of a general awakening is the optimism shining through the midst of doubt and unrest. This optimism is taking the form of illumination, and as the illumination becomes general, fear, anger, doubt, selfishness, and greed pass away. We are anticipating a more general realization of the Truth that is to make men free. That there may be one man or on woman who shall first realize this Truth in the new era is barely possible, but the preponderance of evidence is for a more general awakening to the light of illumination.

Everything which we hold in our consciousness for any length of time becomes impressed upon our subconsciousness and so becomes a pattern that the creative energy will weave into our life and environment. This is the secret of the power of prayer.

The operation of this law has been known to a few in all ages, but nothing was more improbable than the unauthorized revelation of this information by any student of the great esoteric schools of philosophy. This was true because those in authority were afraid that an unprepared public mind might not be ready to make the proper use of the extraordinary power which the application of these principles disclosed.

We know that the universe is governed by law; that for every effect there must be a cause, and that the same cause under the same conditions will invariably produce the same effect. Consequently, if prayer has ever been answered, it will always be answered if the proper conditions are complied with. This must necessarily be true; otherwise, the universe would be a chaos instead of a cosmos. The answer to prayer is therefore subject to law, and this law is definite, exact, and scientific, just as are the laws governing gravitation and electricity. An understanding of this law takes the foundation of Christianity out of the realm of superstition and credulity and places it upon the firm rock of scientific understanding.

The Creative Principle of the Universe makes no exception, nor does it act through caprice of from anger, jealousy, or wrath; neither can it be cajoled, flattered, nor moved by sympathy nor petition; but when we understand our unity with this Universal Principle, we shall appear to be favoured because we shall have found the source of all wisdom and power.

It must be conceded by every thinking person that the answer to prayer furnishes the evidence of an all-pervasive, omnipotent intelligence that is imminent in all things and all persons. We have heretofore personalized this ever-present intelligence and called it God, but the idea of personality has become associated with form and form is a product of matter. The ever-present intelligence or mind must be the Creator of all form, the director of all energy, the source of all wisdom.

In order to secure the best thought of the world on the value of prayer, "The Walker Trust" recently offered a prize of $100.00 for the best essay on "Prayer: The meaning, the reality, and the power of prayer; its place and value to the individual, the church, the state, in the every day affairs of life, in the healing of disease, in times of distress and national danger, and in relation to national ideals and to the world progress."

In response to the invitation, 1,667 essays were received. They came from every quarter of the globe. They were written in nineteen languages. The prize of $100.00 was awarded to the Rev. Samuel McComb, D.D., of Baltimore, MD. A comparative study of these essays is published by the Macmillan Company of New York. In giving his impressions, Mr. David Russell of the Walker Trust says, "To practically all the contributors, prayer is something real and of inestimable value, but unfortunately there is little information given as to the method by which the law is placed in operation."

Mr. Russell himself agrees that the answer to prayer must be the operation of a Natural Law. He says, "We know that to make use of a Natural Law, the intelligence must be able to comprehend its conditions and to direct or control its sequences. Can we doubt that to an intelligence great enough to encompass the spirit, there would be revealed a realm of spiritual law?" It seems that we are rapidly coming into an understanding of this law and understanding its control.

The value of prayer depends upon the law of spiritual activity. Spirit is the Creative Principle of the Universe and is Omnipotent, Omniscient, and Omnipresent. Thinking is a spiritual activity and consists of the reaction of the Individual against the Universal Mind. "I think, therefore I am." When "I cease to think, I cease to exist." Thinking is the only activity that spirit possesses. Spirit is creative, thinking therefore is a creative process; but as the larger part of our thinking processes are subjective rather than objective, most of our creative work is carried on subjectively. But because this work is spiritual work, it is none the less real. We know that all the great eternal forces of Nature are invisible rather than visible, spiritual rather than material, and subjective rather than objective.

But exactly because thinking is a creative process, most of us are creating destructive conditions: we are thinking death rather than life; we are thinking lack rather than abundance; we are thinking disease rather than health; we are thinking inharmony rather than harmony; and our experiences and the experiences of our loved ones eventually reflect the attitude of Mind which we habitually entertain, for be it known that if we can pray for those we love, we can also injure them by entertaining and harboring destructive thoughts concerning them. We are free moral agents and may freely choose what we think, but the result of our thought is governed by an immutable law—this is the modern scientific phraseology for the spiritual statement:

> Be not deceived for God is not mocked, whatsoever a man soweth, that shall he also reap.

Prayer is thought in the form of a petition and an affirmation is a statement of Truth and, when reinforced by Faith (another powerful form of thought), they become invincible, because "Faith is the substance of things hoped for, the evidence of things not seen." This substance is spiritual substance which contains within itself the Creator and the Created, the germ, the Elohim—that which enters in, goes forth, and becomes one with its object.

But prayers and affirmations are not the only forms of creative thought. The architect,. when he plans to erect a wonderful new building, seeks the quiet of his studio, calls on his imagination for new or novel features embodying additional comforts or utilities, and is seldom disappointed in the results.

The engineer who designs to span a chasm or river, visualizes the entire structure before making any attempt to embody it in form. This visualization is the mental image that precedes and predetermines the character of the structure that will eventually take form in the objective world.

The chemist seeks the quiet of his laboratory and then becomes receptive to the ideas from which the world will eventually profit by some new comfort or luxury.

The financier retires to his office or counting room and concentrates on some problem in organization or finance and soon the world learns of another coordination of industry requiring millions of additional capital.

Imagination, Visualization, and Concentration are all spiritual faculties and are all creative, because spirit is the one Creative Principle of the Universe, and he who has found the secret of the creative power of mind has found the secret of the ages. The law stated in scientific terms is that "thought will correlate with its object," but unfortunately, the large majority are allowing their thoughts to dwell upon lack, limitation, poverty, and every other form of destructive thought, and as the law is no respecter of persons, these things become objectified in their environment.

Finally, there is love, which is also a form of thought. Love is nothing material and yet no one will deny that it is something very real. St. John tells us that "God is Love"; again he says, "Now are we all sons of God?" which means that Love is the Creative Principle of the Universe and St. Paul tells us "In Him we live and move and have our being."

Love is a product of the emotions. The emotions are governed by the solar plexus and the sympathetic nervous system. It is therefore a subconscious activity and is entirely under the control of the involuntary system of nerves. For this reason, it is frequently actuated by motives that are dictated neither by reason nor intellect. Every political demagogue and religious revivalist takes advantage of this principle—they know that if they can arouse the emotions, then the result is assured, so that the demagogue always appeals to the passions and prejudices of his audience, never to the reason. The revivalist always appeals to the emotions through the love nature and never to the intellect. They both know that when the emotions are aroused, intellect and reason are stilled.

Here we find the same result obtained through opposite polarities—one appealing to hatred, revenge, class prejudices, and jealousy; the other appealing to love, service, hope, and joy; but the principle is the same. One attracts, the other repels; one is constructive, the other destructive; one is positive, the other negative; the same power is being placed in operation in the same way, but for different purposes. Love and hatred are simply the opposite polarities of the same force, just as electricity or any other force may be used for destructive purposes just as readily as it may be used for constructive purposes.

Some will say that if God is Spirit and is Omnipotent and Omnipresent, how can He be responsible for destructive conditions? He cannot bring about disaster, want, disease, and death. Certainly not, but we can bring these things upon ourselves by a non-compliance with the spiritual laws. If we do not know that thought is creative, we may entertain thoughts of inharmony, lack, and disease, which will eventually result in the conditions of which these thoughts are the seed forms; but by an understanding of the law we can reverse the process and thereby bring about a different result. Good and evil are thereby seen to be but relative terms indicating the result of our thoughts and actions. If we entertain constructive thoughts only, the result will benefit ourselves or others, this benefit we call good; if, on the other hand, we entertain destructive thought, this will result in inharmony for ourselves and others, this inharmony we call evil, but the power is the same in either event. There is but one source of power and we can use the power for good or for evil, just as we can make use of electricity for light, heat, or power by an understanding of the laws governing electricity; but if we are careless of ignorant of the laws governing electricity, the result may be disastrous. The power is not good in one case and evil in the other; the good or evil depend upon our compliance with the law.

Many will ask, "How does this thought agree with the scripture?" Many millions of Bibles are sold annually, and every discovery in chemistry, science, or philosophy must be in agreement with the vital Truth of religious thought.

What, then, was the thought of the Master concerning the Creator? It will be remembered that the question was put to him by a lawyer: "Master, what shall I do to inherit eternal life?" Did He evade the question? Did He quote some ancient authority? Did He recommend some creed or theological dogma? He did not. His answer was direct and to the point:

> Thou shalt love the Lord thy God with all thy heart, with all thy soul, with all thy mind, and with all thy strength; and thy neighbor as thyself.

Where is the God which the lawyer is told to love? Jesus refers to Him as the Father. "He that hath seen me hath seen the Father," again, "The Father and I are one," again, "It is not I that doeth the work, but the Father that dwelleth in me, He doeth the work," again, He taught His disciples to pray, "Our Father which art in Heaven," and when asked concerning the location of Heaven, He said, "Men shall not say Lo here or Lo there, for behold the Kingdom of Heaven is within you."

Here then is authority as to the immanence of the Creator, the Father, from the Master Physician himself. Thus, we find that science and Religion are not in conflict and that within the Church and without there is a setting aside of traditional creeds and a return to the things that the Great Teacher taught and the things for which he stood.

The Old Testament has much to say concerning the God of Jacob and of Moses, but this conception of an anthropomorphic God is principally interesting as indicating the thought of a people who believed that the world was flat, that the sun moved—when science was but magic and religion the dogma of the scholastics.

This was the result of the deductive method of reasoning which originated with certain statements of fact which were universal and absolute, and which were incapable of verification. All other facts must be arrived at by a process of deduction from these original axioms. If facts were observed which seemed to contradict the deductions from which these original axioms were formulated, so much the worse for the facts, they could not be facts. Facts are nothing compared with "statements of Truth" as given by the scholastics. If there were those who persisted in seeing these unwelcome facts, there was the hemlock or the stake or the cross.

But in the New Testament, all of this is reversed. The doctrine of the immanence of God is taught. An objective God is converted into a subjective God. We are told that, "In Him we live and move and have our Being," we are told that "The Kingdom of Heaven is within you," and we are led to infer that God is always in the "Kingdom."

It will readily be seen that the Nazarene completely reversed the process of thought in vogue at that time. Instead of using the deductive method of thinking, he used the inductive. He accepted no authority, no dogma, no creed. Instead of reasoning from the seem to the unseen, the visible to the invisible, from things temporal to things eternal, He reversed this process completely, and as the idea of this immanent God took hold of man, as they began to understand that, "Closer is He than breathing, nearer than hands or feet," then gradually came an awakening, which marks the birth of a splendor such as had never before been known.

In this connection it is interesting to note that the miscellaneous collection of manuscripts which have finally been put together and called the Bible were written by many different men, of many different locations, and at widely different times. At first these manuscripts were circulated separately, later they were collected into a single volume, and for a long time there were serious disputes among the ancient Jews and the early Church Ecclesiastics as to what manuscripts should have a place in the sacred book. In fact, until quite recently there were many of these manuscripts included which are not now to be found in the Bible as recognized by the Protestant Church of today.

The manuscripts comprising the Old Testament were written

originally in Hebrew, those of the New Testament in Greek, and not a single original manuscript of any book either of the Old or the New Testament is in existence today, nor have they been in existence for hundreds of years. We have then only copies of copies of copies many times removed from the original.

When we remember that those who undertook to translate these manuscripts into the English language for the purpose of giving them to the people met with violent opposition, frequently being driven from the country and excommunicated form the church, we see that there was little uniformity in the various translations of these manuscripts which are now called the Bible or the "Word of God."

The King James edition which finally became popular with the people was the work of fifty-four churchmen who agreed with each other that all differences of opinion should be settled at special meetings to be held from time to time and that all marginal notes concerning Greek or Hebrew text should be eliminated. The fact that this edition had the sanction of the King was probably the determining factor in favour of its general adoption, but aside from this the work came to be held in high esteem by the scholastics because of the smoothness and beauty of the diction, the churchman who had the revision in charge evidently sacrificing accuracy for euphony and rhetoric.

And now we have a strictly "American" Bible, the work of the American Revision Committee in which the famous definition of Faith by St. Paul, "Now Faith is the substance of things hoped for, the evidence of things not seen," is changed to "Now Faith is the assurance of things hoped for, a conviction of things not seen," from which it would appear that Paul did not begin to have the insight, the vision, the intuition with which he had been credited, the latter translation completely nullifying and destroying what has heretofore been the most wonderful definition of faith ever given to the world.

If the inductive method of reasoning obtained in religion were put into practice, we should find all religions cooperating for the purpose of bringing about "Peace on Earth and good will toward men." We should find every of theology cooperating with every other school for the purpose of spreading the "glad tidings of great joy," telling of a Redeemer who has come "That we might have life and have it more abundantly," and that this abundant life may be had by looking within instead of without. That objective peace is the result of subjective peace, that harmony without is the natural consequence which follows harmony within, that "men do not gather figs from thistles, or grapes from thorns," and that a man's character is the evidence of the value of his religion: "For by their fruits shall they be known," such a religion satisfies the brain as well as the heart. Religion is to love justice, to long for the right, to love mercy, to forget wrongs and remember benefits, to love the truth, to be sincere, to love liberty, to cultivate the mind, to be familiar with the mighty thoughts that genius has expressed, the noble deeds of the world, to cultivate courage and cheerfulness. To make other happy, to receive new truths with gladness, to cultivate hope, to see the calm beyond the storm, the dawn beyond the night. This is the religion of reason, the creed of science.

PART TWENTY-FOUR

COMPARATIVE RELIGION

COMPARATIVE RELIGION

The primitive races never developed sufficiently to embody their ideas in a literature. They are the so-called savage and barbarous tribes of ancient and modern times and may be known to some extent through the survival of their ideas and customs, through their civilized descendants, and through writings of these same descendants.

In the early period we are impressed by the psychological unity of man. Details of these early races differ, of course, yet the variations are far less than one would suspect, for it is a surprising fact that in all parts of the world the minds of men, as they reach to the fundamental facts of existence, work very nearly in the same way.

The psychological likeness of the process of man's mind is one of the most striking discoveries of modern times.

The essential part of the religions of antiquity is not so much one of belief as of practice—man had not yet evolved enough to reason—to weigh and compare his thoughts. He needed discipline to train his body and his emotions; he was therefore given exercises suitable for this purpose. His struggle for existence caused him to look up to supernatural Beings, whom he designated as Gods, to secure aid. To avert their anger, he must make sacrifices; Gods were to be feared.

Life after death is another universal belief. Some souls went to the Underworld, some to Heaven. Another belief was called *animism*, or the belief that everything—not only animals, but the trees, the thunder, water, earth, fire, etc.—had a spirit or soul.

Spirits might wreak their vengeance on man of they became displeased with his actions, so these in turn were to be feared.

This fear system was allowed, for by it man learned to obey orders. Many tribes had ideas, such as that inanimate parts of an animal (as bones, claws, tails, feet, etc.) retained something of the power of the living thing and this was called *fetishism*.

Closely related to fetishism was *idol worship*. We therefore see that social organizations down to this day are affected by ancient conceptions entertained of the Gods.

Man thought at that time of the Earth as a Goddess—the mother of inexhaustible fertility—of thunder—as warriors' bolts.

These conceptions, we readily admit, color all of our literature and are the origin of many superstitions.

Totemism is a name given to the system of tribal subdivisions, denoted by *totem*. Totems are usually natural objects, such as animals, but also trees and plants, as the emblem of a clan or tribe.

Totem is an American Indian word denoting "ancestor" or "family history", yet the practice exists in many parts of the world. Sacrifice has always been offered in all parts of the world.

In these primitive religions, all so-called civilized religions have had their roots. Some substance of a tree comes through its roots, more comes from the air through its leaves, so civilized religions owe much to the inheritance of the remote uncivilized past.

Their beliefs are often irrational and their practices revolting, but through them the way outward and upward is opened.

Since humanity has never reached perfection, so no religion has ever been a perfect religion, and religion has always suffered from the attempts to crystallize it into form. But all religions are fundamentally the same, they are but the innate desire of the ego of humanity, through its long journey from the clod to deepen faith by adding to faith knowledge.

Man has ever been religious in his nature. There has ever been within him an eternal urge that has pushed him on in his threefold unfoldment—and that something is within itself. It is the Life Principle—and so we might call religion the *Technique of Unfolding Life*.

We are now living in a period of time called by students of the higher thought "the Aryan Period." This is the fifth period of time in world history. Through the other four periods, man was busy with his unfoldment and the acquirement of his faculties. A religion suitable to his meager understanding was a necessary means to this end.

As "man is the heir to the ages," we find that in each primitive period, there were teachings that were handed down to later periods and incorporated into their beliefs. Thus, we have the legends and folk lore stories that still come to us from the long past ages.

As we read and compare these far away traditions and legends, it is interesting to note that through them have come the story of the serpent, the story of the separation of the sexes as Adam and Eve, the story of the Garden of Eden, and the story of an Egg, which is to this day an emblem of life. Many other similar stories are given in modern religions as emblems of Truth.

There was also, always in each, a story of a flood, and this is important because it coincides with science, which says that the earth has been inundated many times.

Babylonia, Assyria, and Egypt have all left legacies of thought and philosophy that have had an influence on the human heart and mind.

But who has not read of that wonderland of Egypt?—and having read, did not feel an at-one-ment with old Egypt and did not have a mystical longing to be there that he might feel this at-one-ment deeper?

This mighty land of a lost romance was in reality created out of a desert by the thrice romantic river Nile.

Here is, perhaps, one of the earth's oldest civilizations. History is lost in the dim far away past, but far beyond 5,000 years B.C., there were tribes whose many Gods were living there and each tribe had their "Totems."

As the neighboring nations had their "Gods of fertility," so their more popular Gods were Osiris and his sister wife Isis. Osiris was represented by the Nile and Isis by the land of Egypt, and at certain seasons the Nile overflowed and irrigated the otherwise desert land, which by the overflow yielded a plentiful harvest, and the harvest represented Horus, the Child God.

Egypt's Gods were many, yet as time wore on, her ideas and ideals changed somewhat and her Gods were grouped, as in families, and finally numbered Nine, which later was called by the Greek an "Eunead." This grouping was because of our numerical system of nine digits.

The effects of this religion was felt in a development of a sensitive social consciousness. It became an age of reflection and philosophical study.

Egypt was however becoming skeptic. In its early days, it was only the kings who ascended to heaven. "Now," they asked, "why not the common man as well?" Here we see the seeds of democracy sprouting.

It was said that there arose a king who was intensely religious and who tried to bring man's mind to the One God idea. This idea was embraced in the God "Ra"—a Sun God, but Egypt was not yet prepared for such an innovation and clung to her old Gods.

Under Rameses II and Seti I, Egypt came under Asiatic influence, but the deities Baal and Anah-Ashtar left no deep impression upon Egyptian beliefs.

PART TWENTY-FIVE

The GREAT RELIGIOUS GROUPS

JUDAISM

The famous land of Palestine, a long narrow strip of country possessing many fertile valleys and high mountains, lies east of the Mediterranean Sea and west of the Arabian Desert. It is 70 miles wide by 125 miles in length—about as large in area as the state of Missouri.

Within it is the Dead Sea, 1,300 feet below sea level, and in it is also Mount Hermon, rising 9,166 feet above sea level and covered with snow from November to August.

This remarkable land and its varied climates played an heroic part in the birth of the religion that has had much influence upon the world.

The early books of the Bible were written much later than is generally supposed, and the collection of the Hebrew Patriarch stories in the Book of Genesis consists largely of traditions of a later tribal history.

It is indicated by tradition that the early Hebrew nations were composed of four tribes, which were said to be descended from four mothers and of which two are considered of importance: the "Leah" and the "Rachel" tribes. (Leah mean "wild cow" and Rachel mean an "ewe.")

Opinions differ as to whether these were totems or economic symbols. The Leah tribe might have been cattle raisers, while the Rachel tribe sheep raisers. The time is recorded at about 1,300 B.C. It was probably the Rachel tribe only that were in Egypt and were later led out by Moses.

Reasoning by analogy, it is probable that the religion of these tribes before they entered Palestine did not differ materially from that of the other tribes about them, for the primitive Semitic Pillars, circumcision, the harem, etc. were perpetuated by them into much later times. It is then reasonable to think their religion similar to that of those around them. Each tribe may have had its deity; we read of the God "Gad" that was probably the God of the tribe of Asher, the Goddess Ashera. The Kenite God was "Yahweh", or Jehovah, and ancient Hewbrew writers say this worship went back to earliest times.

This early God was like many others of that age, thought to be a God of Fertility and was said to mean "He who causes passionate love." They attributed all activity to him, like the eruption of a volvano, victories over their enemies, etc.

There are indications that "Yahweh" may have been a Divine name in North Arabia for thousands of years before Moses and that the roaming emigrants from this region to Babylonia and Palestine had carried this name and worship to those countries.

Perhaps the greatest figure in all this history was Moses, born and reared in Egypt while the Hebrew Nation was held in bondage. There, he was the adopted son of a Princess who brought him up in all the learning of Egypt. But seeing the oppression of his people, it is recorded that he slew an Egyptian one day and then, in fear of vengeance, fled from Egypt to the country of the Medianites-Kenites and lived there many years.

While there, he married Jethro's daughter. Jethro was a Priest of Yahweh. At the "Burning Bush" on Yahweh's volcanic mountain, he was so impressed with the power and majesty of Yahweh as to become a follower. He returned to Egypt to preach to his enslaved people a way of escape through this same power of Yahweh.

The escape was made and at the Burning Mountain a "Covenant" was made to make Yahweh their God and to serve Him. Later, Moses and his brother Aaron were made Priests, and the covenant was placed in a box or Ark that could be easily carried from place to place and which contained the sacred emblems, which were emblematic of Yahweh's presence with them.

His new worshipers' duties were summed up into a code of ten laws—today known as the "Ten Commandments," thought by most people to be ten because this infant race could count them on their fingers. This was a moral code of laws with a strict mathematical basis and, what is most remarkable, this code has stood the test of the ages and still holds good and is embodied in the laws of most countries of the earth today.

It is true that the contemporary religions and later ones had in them practically most of the laws given to Moses, but somehow these have stood out clear and have been used by all nations as a basis for law.

Yahweh's emphatic demand of the "One God" idea, or monotheism, was the first great ethical teaching. Next was for righteousness between man and man. His first Prophets held to the idea of sacrifice and justice. Later ones told of Yahweh's love. "Yahweh had chosen Israel for a bride" and her faithlessness to him was base ingratitude, and deeply grieved his heart.

Later prophets spoke of a new teacher to come—of a Messiah—and of a change of heart and an inwardness of religion—and the teachings of the Prophets Isaiah and Jeremiah did much to set religion free from time worn shackles.

The development of Israel's religion, from its primitive Semitic beginning to the formation of Judaism, is one of the most significant chapters in human history. For in other countries as in Egypt, the monotheistic idea was grasped by but a few. In Israel alone was it made the possession of the people. It is on account of this that the Hebrew Religion became mother to three great monotheistic religions of the world: Judaism, Mohammedanism, and Christianity.

Jerusalem was "Yahweh's Holy City" and is to this day. But to follow the Hebrews, who are later called Jews, through their long history of rises and falls, of their captivity and return, of their national evolution, and then their final "scattering among nations," is not our purpose.

Man has always been a roving animal, and coming in contact with other nations led to national troubles. We read of friction between the Jews and the Samaritans, and later with Persia and Babylonia, and Greece and Rome, and then they felt the influence of the various currents of life and thought that swayed the world.

The Sages and Seers, Philosophers and Poets of these foreign nations had their weight, and we see the result in the Proverbs of Solomon and the Psalms of David, and note the Greek thought in the Book of Ecclesiastes.

MOHAMMEDANISM

The city of Mecca was the seat of a powerful tribe of Koreisch people and was a place to which all the people of Arabia came each year to celebrate a festival or to trade.

It was under these conditions that Mohammed was born in Mecca, 570 A.D.

Before his birth, a sect had broken away from the old religion and claimed to be seeking for the faith of Abraham.

Mohammed seems to have been much given to Mystical and religious things. He lived in Mecca until he was 50 years old, having in the meantime married and had six children, two sons and four daughters. At one time he was agitated by grave doubts and, withdrawing from his family and Mecca, spent two years in a cave in prayer and meditation, and at the end came back with a strong conviction that God had commissioned him to be a prophet to his people and he at once began and continued preaching for ten years during which period he attracted but few followers. These, however, were loyal ones—and in time the number grew.

His cardinal doctrine was the "Oneness" and "Aloneness" of God.

This God he called "Allah" meaning "The God."

He saw God as a Great Human Being or a transcendent man—He had hands, feet, eyes, and all other human attributes.

He was all-wise and powerful and an absolute despot of the world.

It was useless for man to try to understand him, but He would be merciful if man submitted to His will.

The next doctrine to be taught was that Mohammed was His Prophet—"No prophet was to come after Mohammed." Religion was to give man peace, the Arabic root of which is "Salama," said to be the infinitive of the causative stem of which is "Islam," "to submit." As he preached the doctrine of Submission, he called his religion "Islam."

As time went on he added to these doctrines many material teachings as reward and punishment. Believers were to be rewarded with a material paradise in the way of a Harem Home and unbelievers were to be tortured in a very material Hell. Two passages from the Koran illustrate this:

> Is the reward of Goodness, aught but goodness? Then which of your Lord's bounties will ye deny? and besides these are gardens twain—with green foliages—in each are gushing springs—in each fruits and palms and Pomegranates—In them are maidens best and fairest—bright and large-eyed maidens, kept in their tents, reclining in cushions and beautiful carpets—Blessed be the name of the Lord, possessed of honour and majesty.
> (Koran-Sura LV 060-75)

So much for the rewards, but also note these punishments:

> To those who misbelieve, for them are cut out garments of fire—Then shall be poured over their heads boiling water—wherewith what is in their bellies shall be dissolved and their skins, too, and for them are maces of iron, whenever they desire to come forth therefrom through pain, they are sent back into it, and taste ye the torment of the Burning.
> (Koran-Sura XXII, 20)

The doctrines of angels and Satan were borrowed from Judaism.

On account of some dislike by the people of Mecca for Mohammed, he fled from there to Medina. This is a great point in Mohammedanism, for from this, their time is marked. At Medina, Mohammed was accepted as their ruler and in it Islam was changed somewhat.

For some time as had been his custom, he continued to pray with his face toward Jerusalem, for he fondly hoped that the Jews, of which there were many in Medina, would accept him as a successor of their prophets. In this he was sadly disappointed.

He then changed the direction of prayer from Jerusalem to

Mecca—and the ideals of Arabia soon became more influential than those of Jerusalem and Israel.

ZOROASTRIANISM

If we read of some of the oder religions with the idea of seeing what the people of that religion believed, we may get a wrong idea or concept of that belief, because the time and the locality are an important indication of its teachings.

Zoroastrianism was born in Persia, a great table-land country about one-fifth the area of the United States. It is almost surrounded by high mountains, which open only through rocky passes. It has but few rivers and these lose themselves in the sandy soil.

As Zoroaster was said to be the great agricultural God, we can more readily see why agriculture became a part of religious duty.

The struggle with nature in this elevated table-land produced an efficient and practical people, not unlike the Romans in general characteristics. But note the difference of their kinsmen in India, where there was a milder climate. Here you see the speculative, contemplative, and highly mystical character; but the Persian remained to the end an active and alert body, more interested in things objective than metaphysical. So to them was sent a Teacher and Master who could reach their minds, hearts, and abilities—and Zoroaster's teachings are quite different from all others.

The book of the "Avestas", or "Knowledge", was written long after Zoroaster's days, but it carries his teachings and ideals in the form of poems (not unlike our psalms). They composed their religion.

The old Iranian religion still held sway and while Zoroaster opposed these, Ahura under Zoroaster became "Ahura-Mad-Masdah," a fire God. So he taught Astronomy to his people with the fire of the Sun as the life of all living things.

Zoroaster was at first called Zarathustra. The names are no doubt indicative of office rather than person, like our word "president" or "judge", but it is certain there was one great Zoroaster, one with new ideals and a system.

At about twenty years of age he retired from his fellows and sought his own Faith and no doubt began to formulate the general truths of his system; and again like Jesus, we see him at 30 years of age getting visions and revelations.

In a vision that was thrice repeated in one day, he was admitted to the presence of Ahura-Masdah, the Supreme Being Himself, and was taught by Him in Heaven.

Upon Zoroaster's return to earth, he at once began to preach to the then ruling Priests his own religion, the worship of Masdah, the glorification of Archangels, denouncing demons, etc.

Later, he was given six more visions, in which each of the Archangels appeared to him and each of these became to him personified qualities, such as "Good Thought", "Good Words", "Good Deeds", etc.

Zoroaster was a practical Monotheist. In his thought, Ahura-Masdah was the one God Supreme.

He was diplomatic in that he incorporated or so used the ideals with new interpretations as to lessen the offense and shock to his new converts.

He taught that man had two natures: an animal and a Divine nature. Through practice of good thoughts, "Perfect Righteousness," etc., man would be one at last with Masdah, and to those who were trying, Masdah gave help, if asked to do so.

He assumed that man is the arbiter of his own destiny; he can do right if he will.

Right is truthfulness, the practice of justice, and the fostering of agriculture.

Wrong is lying, robbery, and the destruction of irrigation, cattle, or crops.

Rewards and punishments were alike the results of these acts.

The Vedic Religion

India, extending from the Himalaya Mountains on the North to the Indian Ocean on the South, presents a variety of temperatures and climate. It is a great three-cornered country, 1,000 miles North and South and almost the same distance East and West.

The scene of the Vedic religion, however, is only concerned with the two great river valleys of the Indus and the Ganges. In the upper part of the valley of the Indus, where the rivers are fed by the melting of the snows on the Himalayas, the climate is that of a temperate zone, much like that of our Central States. The valley of the Ganges lies further to the South and is dependent for its fertility upon the rains brought over by the monsoons. The climate is not favourable to human life and the struggle for existence is severe.

There came into the upper Indus valley, through the passes of the Kush Mountains, some tribes of the Aryan stock. They spread over the northern part of the Indus valley and lived there for some centuries, and here were composed the Vedas, a sort of Bible or Epic of Divine Wisdom. Later, some of this race passed into the Ganges valley, and some writers hold that the splitting of the religions that followed was due to the depressing effect of the climate of that valley.

More than one hundred books are called *Vedas*, the principal of which are the *Rig-Veda*, the *Yagur-Veda*, and the *Sama-Veda*. Veda means "wit" or "knowledge". The oldest of the Vedas is the Rig-Veda, which consists of hymns of praise containing about 10,000 stanzas, though not all are stanzas of praise—some are called family books, some are Books of Blessings and Curses, etc.

They are supposed to have been composed by different poets and seers. The other Vedas were dedications and some were set to music.

The *Brahmanas* are theological treatises written in prose and deal with sacrificial ceremonies. They often reveal a reflective spirit that was unsatisfied with the mere offering of animal sacrifices and sought for union with a spiritual Being.

Closely connected with the Brahmanas' reflective side are the

Upanishads, which are a new and quite different religion. The Upanishads as literature are of next importance to the Rig-Vedas.

It is generally agreed that the Upanishads were written before the time of Gautama, called the Buddha, who died 487 B.C., and this seems certain because the whole Buddhistic system of thought presupposes the philosophic conceptions of the Upanishads. It is therefore reasonable that Brahmanas and Upanishads developed in the period 800 to 500 B.C.

The Rig-Veda was more like a social order—a simple patriarchal society ruled by chieftains called Rajas.

In Rig-Veda, the family was the foundation of society. The father, the Lord of the house, was also a priest who offered sacrifice; the wife, thought subjected to him, occupied a position of greater honour than in the age of the Brahmanas, for she took part in the offering of the sacrifice, she was the mistress of the house, and shared control of the children, the slaves, and the unmarried brothers and sisters of the husband.

The standards of morality were high.

The community was agricultural and the standard of value was a cow, though the metals gold and bronze are referred to. Later, conquests were made by aborigines of other countries, especially in the Ganges valley, and in the course of struggles thus entailed there came about a difference of occupation and eventually there was a priestly class, a warrior class, and an agricultural class, and here is the beginning of the caste systems of those countries.

Of the Vedic Deities, it was claimed there were thirty-three, a very significant number in human evolution, but the most important was *Indra*, who was a tribal God supposed to be the fighter of the national battles—and this fighting character he has never thrown off. He is of the earth—earthy. He slays dragons and monsters. He was a glutton, a drunkard, and a boaster. Another God was Agui, God of Fire.

(It is well here to stop and consider the remarkable fact that in nearly all of these early religions, this consideration of the Sacredness of the four elements—Earth, Air, Water, and Fire. This is a universal teaching of those early religions and is the same in all parts of the world. These ancient people of India manifested a strong lust towards the multiplication of Gods through personification of the powers of Nature and of the Morning and the Evening stars, or Sun and Moon, and Mother Earth, etc.)

In the Rig-Veda, the Creation is referred to as an act of natural Generation (Rig-Veda, IV-2).

The king of Death was called *Yama* and ruled over the places of the dead, both good and bad.

Their idea of immortality was very vague, though a strong desire for it is indicated in later literature, the Upanishad and the Mahabharata. There are clear traces of an Indian belief in a Hell and in a Heaven.

The Brahamanas was a book of rituals relating both to sacrifice and to worship, and also to the duties of the four different castes—the "Brahman" or Priestly class, the Rajauya or warrior class, the Viazga or agricultural class, and the Indra or servant class.

BUDDHISM

Like Jesus of Nazareth, Gautama, founder of the Buddhist teachings, has left no books of his own writing to the world, though there are some which include his doctrine that have been ascribed to him.

He was born near Benares about 567 B.C. His father was a prince named Suddhodana.

At the time of his birth, the mother was on her way to her father's home, but her son was born under some tall trees in a pleasant grove, called "Lumbini." The mother died a week later and her sister reared the boy.

It is related that Gautama had little or no interest in his princely duties and in reality abandoned his home, wife, and child to devote his time to study and religion. But this was not unusual, for with the rise of the Upanishads, there had grown up a body of Ascetics who abandoned the world, lived in poverty in forests and mountains, and begged for their food.

Gautama was led to this step by four visions: that of beholding a man decrepit through age; a sick man; a decaying corpse; and a dignified hermit. Before leaving home, he stole into the chamber of his sleeping wife and child to look at them for a last time.

This parting the Buddhists call the "Great Renunciation."

He then went southeast and south of the Ganges, where he spent some time studying the Brahman Philosophy under two dignified teachers. But this did not satisfy him and he withdrew into a jungle and for six years gave himself to the severest asceticism, and thereby gained fame in India.

But still he had no peace of soul until one day, through intensified fasting, he fell in a swoon and was regarded by his disciples as dead; but he recovered and despairing of further profit from such rigorous penance, he began to take regular food and gave up on his self-mortification.

There now followed a second crisis in Gautama's career. All the teachings of Hindu philosophy had failed him, and he almost despaired of reaching his goal.

While wandering and meditating, he sat down under a Banyan tree. Here he reviewed the years of his life and fought with temptation in much the same way as that recorded of Jesus. As the day ended, he saw in a vision a new path and saw that he himself was Buddha, or the "Enlightened One."

This tree was called the "Bo" tree—the tree of enlightenment. His secret was his Peace in the power over the human heart, of inward culture and Love for others.

Because of his experience, the Bo tree has become to the Buddhist almost what the cross is to the Christian. Man has had his symbols for unseen or metaphysical qualities throughout the ages.

He taught the idea of a Supreme God, and that the Devas or Gods of the old religion were real beings, but that they were like men, entangled with the material meshes.

He taught Karma and Reincarnation, or the doctrine of cause and effect.

YOGA SYSTEM

We cannot leave India and her mighty schools of thought without glancing at the modern development and we must turn to history to see how the ancient beliefs became changed.

Neither the Vedic religion nor the Upanishads was supplanted by the Buddhist religion nor by the Jainistic heresies, for each lived on and in turn has undergone many changes in the course of the centuries.

India has had many upheavals and has been subjugated by different people at different periods, as by the Syrians, the Parthenians, and the Mohammedans; but the most important conquest was that by Great Britain in 1803 A.D.

The various systems of philosophy that were evolved out of the thought of the Upanishads maintained that there are two Eternal Beings. This was the theory of the great thinker Kapila, who revolted from the monotheistic theory of the Upanishads and who recognized only matter and the individual soul—he recognized no God.

The Yoga system was still later established by one Patangali. Yoga means "yoke" or "union" and in this case union with God or the higher self, and lays emphasis on experience and knowledge rather than on asceticism, fasting, and other penances that had long been practiced in India. These were taken up and enforced by the Yoga with philosophical explanations and with the object of isolating the soul from matter, that it might be united with God.

To stand with mud caked in the hair of one's head until the birds nested in it, immovable because the soul was in static abstraction, was one of the extreme manifestations of the practice of the yoga philosophy.

Still another development of the Upanishads was that of the "Vedanta," originated by a commentator on the Veda who lived about 800 A.D.

It claims the phenomenal world has no reality of existence any more than that of a dream and that the bad dream of birth and rebirth will go on until each soul recognizes that there is no real existence except *Brahman-Atman*.

Then the knowledge of itself becomes salvation.

Here Brahman sometimes meant God Supreme, and at others a Supreme Personal God. And here is the origin of some of our very recent ideals such as the unreality of matter and the belief that the Supreme God can become personal, as held by some of our Orthodox Churches.

The *Madhabharata*, the great Indian Epic, is a great work of many authors, whose mass of material was a gradual growth and based on stories dating far back into Indian Antiquity. It is a story of many wars, intrigues, hatred, loves, etc., and centers around a hero, Krishna, who was later deified and became a God to the people, who worshipped him as "Bhagavata" or the "Adorable."

The *Bhagavad-Gita*, or Song of the Blessed, lends probability to the theory just mentioned. This story, so popular in this day among advanced students all over the world, is an episode from the sixth book of the Mahabharata. It points out the two natures in man—the lower and the higher self—and that these are ever at war with each other. The teaching is given in dialogue form and Arjuna asks Krishna many questions, to which he replies with much spiritual information and illustration.

In Him, Pantheism is made personal. The great struggle of life is the struggle between one's higher and lower self. There are other epic poems that have much significance in India, as the Ramayama. The teaching in general stands for lofty ideals, while some have more or less degenerated into immorality.

Hinduism is today a religion of nearly 200,000,000 people and presents many varieties of faiths and practices. These diversities have been created by an endless lot of influences, both internal and external, that have come to India at large since the Vedic age. It has left to it some ideas that are beautiful and many noble. But the one great ideal is a mental conception of religion, rather than a spiritual one.

CONFUCIANISM

> Always and in every thing let there be reverence; with the deportment grave, as when one is thinking, and with the speech composed and definite.
>
> — Li-Ki—I-i.

The above is a quotation from one of the old, old Chinese writers, and when one stops to consider the Chinese character of this late day, we know that this teaching has sunken deeply into the Chinese character. There is no race with as much natural dignity, poise, and reverence.

The beginning of Chinese civilization appears to have been in Northwest China in those provinces watered by the Yellow River in a dry and bracing climate, with a productive soil that grows apples, pears, grapes, nuts, and millet.

Modern metaphysics is beginning to see that there is a hidden side to every object in the Universe—and the high initiates of that day probably did not look upon this hidden side as containing a deity to be worshipped, but they did see and teach an unseen quality or spiritual force much the same as we of a later day do.

They account for the origin of the Universe by generation from two souls or "Breaths", called *Yang* and *Yin*. Yang was warmth, light and life, also the Heavens from which all good things come. Yin was darkness, cold, death, also the Earth. Yang was subdivided into a number of good spirits, called *Shen*. Yin was divided into evil spirits called *Kwel*, or specters, and these two kinds of spirits animated the human race.

Birth consisted in the infusion of these souls. Death separated them and the Shen qualities returned to the Yang and the Kwel to the Yin.

As man had one Supreme Ruler, so also the spirit world had a Supreme Ruler. Shang-Ti was the Ruler, but they sacrificed to many lesser rulers nevertheless.

The early religions are based on five canonical books Confucius rescued from the early past of his days and transmitted to posterity:

A book of History, a book of Odes, a book of filial Piety, a book of Changes (Astrology), and a book of Rituals. These teachings have largely made Chinese character what it is to this day.

The Emporer is thought to be the "Son of Heaven" and reverence for ancestors has been a chief feature of instruction. Temples are scattered all over the land and two great festivals were held at the Winter and Summer Solstices, showing that they knew what the esoteric significance of these were.

The most influential person in Chinese history is Confucius, who lived somewhere between 550 to 480 B.C. As records show, his life was similar to that of any ordinary life in any age.

At the age of fifteen, he bent his mind to learning. Later he married and had a child, but domestic life was not congenial and he divorced his wife and became a teacher, and here he found time for study and meditation, two things dear to the mystic soul.

At thirty, he stood firm. He had formed his own opinion and he became famous and drew to himself many youths of noble families as pupils, and it is said that at one time he had 3,000 pupils. He was a strict formalist in all things, never a reformer; but to the end, his religion was that of his ancestors.

The remote past was to him a golden age and to perpetuate it was his aim.

His noblest saying was this:

> That which I do not want others to put upon me, I also wish not to put upon them.

A golden rule, truly telling the ruling principle of this religion, is that the highest aim in heaven and earth is "Virtue, for Virtue's sake" and "Order is Heaven's only law."

Lao-Tzu was a second great teacher and mystic in China. He was born about 600 B.C. He occupied some high position at the imperial court for many years, but when signs of old age began to show on him, he resigned and went into seclusion and there he wrote that remarkable book of wisdom, *The Tao Te Ching*.

This gives the oldest teaching of Lao Tzu. In his system, the great and adorable thing is the Tao, which may be translated as the "Way" or "Power" or "Nature" or even "God."

To Lao Tzu, the Tao seemed the inexpressible infinite. As he expresses in these words:

> He who knows the Tao,
> Does not care to speak of it;
> he who is ever ready to speak about it,
> does not know it.
> How pure and still the Tao is,
> as if it would ever so continue;
> I do not know whose son the Tao is.
> It might appear to have been before Shang-ti.

See in this "the feeling after God" that St. Paul speaks of. Again he says:

> The highest excellence is like that of water. The excellence of water appears in its benefitting all things and in its occupying without striving the low places, which all men dislike. Hence, its way is near to that of the Tao.

All through his works we see a self effacement and a sort of fatalism—Buddhism in its northern form. The Mahayana was brought over into China in about 75 A.D., but knowledge of it had reached there long before and for some centuries no Chinese were allowed to become monks; but as time went on, Chinese students made journeys to India to farther learn of her beliefs.

But Confucianism was ever opposed to that of Buddhism and much internal dissatisfaction was the result, for in Buddhism many found the spiritual something that they needed, and today Chinese Buddhism is nearly akin to that of Tibet. Their beliefs in prayer, in heaven and hell as a place of abodes between incarnations, etc., and so in China we see Confucianism, Taoism, and Buddhism; not exclusive religions, but each affecting the whole.

We find that in summing up that Confucianism ministers to the moral man, Taoism to the problems of the spirit forces that play upon the present life of man, and Buddhism makes vivid the future of life. Confucianism deals with the visible present, Taoism with the invisible present, and Buddhism with the invisible future.

SHINTOISM

Japan is a group of islands off the eastern coast of Asia, which stretch in a curve from about 31° to 45° North latitude. Its early inhabitants were probably of two races, the Aium and the Yamato.

Traditions are about the same as of other neighbouring races. The Yamato conquered most of the territory, but the evolution was slow—the people lived in huts, there were neither cities nor temples, they lived chiefly by hunting and fishing, some crude efforts to raise rice were made, iron implements were used, marriage and the family was only partially organized—but at a later date, evolution was hastened by influence from China—writing was introduced, the Buddhist religious teachings began to have influence, a little later came Confucianism, which has always been more of a material philosophy than that of a spiritual religion—and through this came Japan's state religion.

The "Shint", Japan's Emperors, were always held in thought as descending from two primitive deities who gave birth to all other gods of Japan. The primitive religion was the conception that man, animals, and Gods formed one society. Their word for God was "Kami", meaning "super being". Kami was sometimes applied to the Sun, heavens, or even the winds, also to a serpent; sometimes to jewels, stones, and in fact to any and all things that excite wonder. To them as to the semitic, the mystery of the propagation of life was most marvelous, hence the numerous symbols of phallic worship, but be it said of the Japanese that they saw the higher lesson in phallic symbology and not the lower, for in reverencing the symbolic forms they reverenced the Divine in its most wonderful and beneficent form and it would be well for modern psychologists to forever put from their minds the old idea that any of these object lessons given to men for their upliftment should ever be thought of as a degenerate practice.

Creation was told as a tale of generation by a God and a Goddess, our same positive and negative forces. There was no idea of a soul or of sin, though there was an idea of Heaven and the Underworld; but happy to say, neither of these carried ideas of rewards and punishment. Confucian philosophy brought the great reverence for ancestry and especially that of the rulers. This is called "Shintoism" in Japan as in China and through it the family and marriage became more regulated and these took next rank to that of the Kami. Thus, in Shint's doctrine, man is in this life akin to the Divine and after death joins the company of those who are reverenced. How nearly akin is this idea to our modern Brotherhood of Man as "Sons of God"!

It is said of the Japanese that they pray not for forgiveness of sins, but for the sweet things of life; and for happiness, but not for blessedness; and again it is said, that the worshipper "May be conscious that his heart is not of Divine quality, of purity, but he can of his own accord blow it off like dust or wash it off like a stain and regain its purity." All of which, if analyzed, we find it to be excellent modern psychology.

So today we see in Japan a leading oriental nation. Christianity has made some converts, but Buddhism prevails; while her progressive spirit was probably most fostered by China through Confucius' teachings and there we see more clearly "How man is heir to the nations' gains."

The Philosophy of Greece

The religion of Greece was a religion of music, literature, statuary, and painting. The religious side had in it more philosophy than religion, nevertheless there was a meditative note running through it all, showing that here the human mind began a real analytical review of the vast workings of the universe about it.

The early inhabitants, reaching back to 3,000 B.C. and beginning in the Stone Age, evolved in a similar manner to those of Babylonia, Egypt, and China. Indo-Europeans entered from the north and passed through the valley of the Danube and in turn came under the influence of the Bronze Age. All these mingled and were transformed and absorbed.

The Pantheon was but a fusion of all the deities.

Some of the greater gods were Apollo and Hermes.

In Miletus, an Ionian city in Asia in the sixth century B.C., Thales, Anaximander, and Anaximanes perceived a unity of the world about, but sought for one element that was the origin of all, the transformation of which would account for all.

Thales called it "Water"; Anaximander called it "Air"; but Pythagorus, who probably had studied in Arabia and Babylonia, held that numerical relations explained all things, and we find that even today, this science of numbers is still being taught by teachers of the higher thought.

Other great minds advanced other great ideas. One philosopher held that God is one, not many, and that he was not like men. All things are one and nothing comes into being or is ever destroyed. This philosopher was Xenophanes.

Socrates (469-397 B.C.) was the critic philosopher of his age. He showed the shallowness of much pretended knowledge and at the same time tried to draw men to self-realization. He was preeminently a teacher and his method of teaching by means of questions and answers has never been surpassed. He believed that there was within himself a spirit that would guide him and his idea was to find the best way to live here and now. He lived the simple life, and when condemned to death, died bravely and cheerfully.

Plato, Socrates' pupil for eight years, was one of the world's greatest philosophers, teachers, and authors. He taught that all things outward are subject to ceaseless change, and ideas only are permanent and eternal. That sensuous existences have originated from attempts to express an eternal idea. The soul, in his view, stands midway between ideas and the corporeal world and unites both. The soul belongs to the world above the senses and in it only can we find true and lasting existence.

Aristotle, a pupil of Plato, found reality not in ideas, but in things. "Things are ever changing, but the species remain." His idea of the ruler of the universe was a mind eternal. These great minds were followed by the founders of such schools as the Stoics and the Epicureans.

CHRISTIANITY

Jesus was born in Palestine, which country had been the "Holy Land" of the Jews.

This part of the world was at the time of his birth under Roman government, for Rome had indeed by this time become the "Mistress of the World," but many Jewish officials had charge under the Romans, such as Herod the Great, who was King over this particular domain. It was during his reign that Jesus was born.

His mother, Mary, was wife of the carpenter Joseph. Jesus was brought up to this trade and followed it until he was about thirty years old.

Shortly before he reached that age, his cousin John the Baptist had begun to preach that "the Kingdom of God was at hand" and to baptize men in token of their desire to be ready for its coming. Jesus went to be baptized of John, and as he was coming out of the water, a voice from Heaven spoke to him declaring that he was the "Son of God" and the expected "Messiah". Jesus had been reared among those who shared the belief in the coming of a Messiah who would indeed be not only a spiritual saviour, but would be their king and assist in the restoration of their lost glory as a nation.

The conviction that he was to fulfill these expectations overwhelmed him and he retired to the wilderness to think out what it meant.

The story of his struggle there is told in the narrative of The Temptation, and from this struggle he came forth with a new conception of the Messiahship and of the Kingdom of God.

He put away the political ideal definitely. That ideal involved the establishment of a rule over the body of men by force of arms.

He chose the rule of self-sacrifice and love.

He staunchly held to a Messianic mission, but it was to be one of a spiritual and not of a political realm.

In His teachings concerning this Kingdom, Jesus taught that it is every man's privilege to come under the direct personal guidance of the God within himself, as on occasion he would say to them this, "Said I not unto you, 'Ye are Gods'" and again, "The Kingdom of Heaven is within you." This Kingdom was no longer simply a monarchy with God as a far off sovereign; it was a family of which God was the loving Father and all men were brothers. The heart of his message is told in the parable of the Prodigal Son.

He chose twelve men from the every day, simple walks of life to be his disciples and companions and spent more than a year traveling here and there in their company preaching and healing the sick and when he at last disclosed to them his conception of Messiahship, they could not understand his uncompromising denunciation of sham, his emphasis for personal righteousness.

The light value he set upon ceremonial set those in higher power against him, and finally they accomplished his death through crucifixion.

Jesus himself wrote nothing, but his matchless discourses and his parables—showing his insight into the nature of God and man—were afterwards compiled by his disciples, and are now embodied in our New Testament.

The story of the Christian Church, which was established by the Apostles soon after Jesus had left them, is a long one with which we are more or less familiar. The believers and the Apostles were enthusiastic missionaries and through the three centuries after Jesus' death, succeeded in planting the teachings in many countries around the Mediterranean Sea.

But at Rome in Italy was perhaps the greatest center, and it was there that the great Roman Catholic Church was established and today claims a larger part of the Christian followers.

In the middle centuries, the church became able to assert its power over the state and finally became supreme, in name at least.

About 1,300 A.D., men began to find the need of new ideals, one of which was for more religious liberty, which partially came about through the great religious reformations headed by Martin

Luther and John Calvin. From these came our Protestant churches of the 18th and 19th centuries; and because of a still larger liberty, political as well as religious, our own American Colonies were formed, and here grew and flourished such churches as the Presbyterian, the Methodist, Baptist, and others.

The Religions to Today

Confucius said, for the races a splendid ideal of fine physical attainment—and no hardier, more capable of endurance, race or races exist than those who came within or under his influence.

Almost contemporary to Confucius was the effect of Zoroaster's great agricultural development and his lessons in planetary influence on man and nature, for Nature herself has to be lifted as man is lifted.

Then came the Hebrew race with the idea of sacrifice, and Egypt, with a search for the truth as to immortality, and the working out of the ethics of a new civilization.

Buddha's great message was one of a deeply spiritual nature, teaching men the contemplative side of life as a means to man's ultimate goal.

Greece reached God through her love and creation of the beautiful and is still recognized as the mother of art.

Rome gave us government, both individual and national, and with these great fundamentals acquired by man, he was now ready for another great ideal—and Jesus the Christ came. "For when the pupil is ready, the Master will appear."

In the early part of the 19th century, the religions of the Western world had become a recognized establishment, namely, Catholicism and Protestantism were the two great distinct bodies representing Christianity. By "Western world," we mean not only the Americas, but all of Europe as well.

By this time, though, the "Age of Reason" was stirring men's minds and the indwelling spirit was also stirring some few to the working of nature's invisible forces round and about us.

In Europe, philosophy and scientific research flew to what was for the first time very dizzy heights, and in America at around 1850 A.D. much investigation began.

A craving for a more definite knowledge as to the soul's immortality led to the great wave of what is now called "spiritualism" and the organization of a church by this name. But like all religions, it has suffered from many perversions of its real purpose.

Contemporaneous with the rise of spiritualism, there were other ideals being advanced. The old time, or Christ form of healing, was revived and then that great modern American seer, poet and prophet Ralph Waldo Emerson, began swaying men's minds and lifting them to spiritual heights heretofore undreamed of.

Then came Christian Science and the New Thought movements that have been the means of spiritual and mental unfoldment. And then another great awakening occurred when Madame Helen P. Blavatsky came with her old and new message of the "Secret Doctrines" of the Buddhist faith, from which was established the Theosophical Society and which has even at this early time been a means of many modifications in the New Thought Movement.

INDEX

A

B

C

D

E

F

G

H

T

U

V

W

Y

Z

BIOGRAPHY OF CHARLES F. HAANEL

Charles F. Haanel was born in Ann Arbor, Michigan on May 22, 1866. He received many degrees, including hon. Ph.D., College National Electronic Institute; Metaphysics, Psy. D., College of Divine Metaphysics; and M.D., Universal College of Dupleix, India. He is the ex-President of the Continental Commercial Company and the ex-President of the Sacramento Valley Improvement Company.

He is the author of works on philosophy, psychology, causation, science of living, personality, and science of mind, synthesized in *The Master Key System*, a system of philosophy for application to the affairs of everyday life.

Mr. Haanel was affiliated with many groups, including Fellow London College of Psychotherapy; member Authors' League of America; American Society of Psychical Research; member of the Society of Rosicrucians; the American Suggestive Therapeutical Association; Science League of America; Pi Gamma Mu Fraternity; Master Mason, Keystone Lodge No. 243, A.F. & A.M.; created a Noble in Moolah Temple.

Mr. Haanel died on November 27, 1949 at the age of 83. He was buried in Bellefontaine Cemetery, St. Louis.

For more information, visit **www.haanel.com**.

KALLISTI

“THE BOOKS YOU NEED

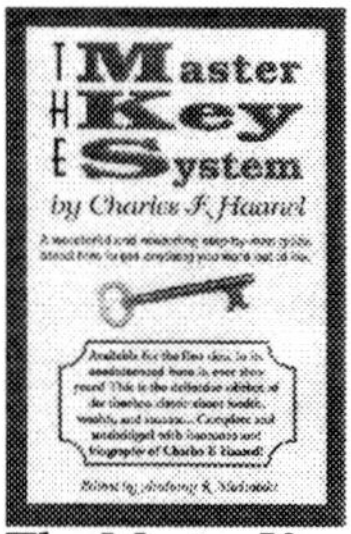

The Master Key System
Charles F. Haanel

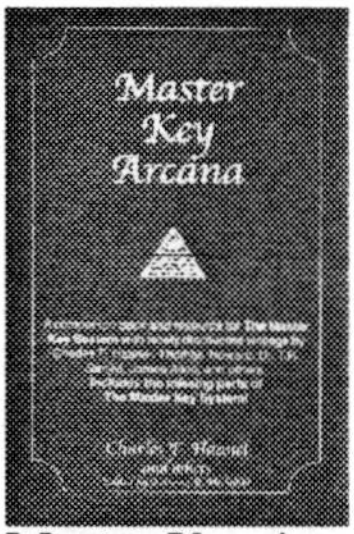

Master Key Arcana
Charles F. Haanel
& others

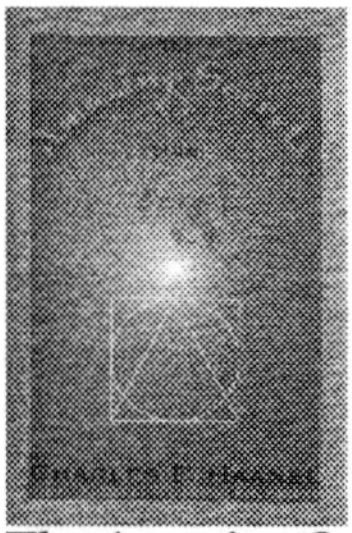

The Amazing Secrets the Yogi
Charles F. Haanel

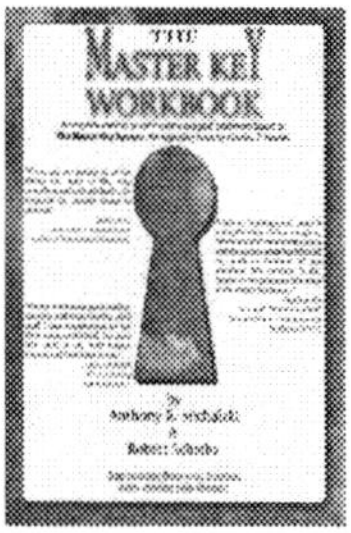

The Master Key Workbook
Tony Michalski
& Robert Schmitz

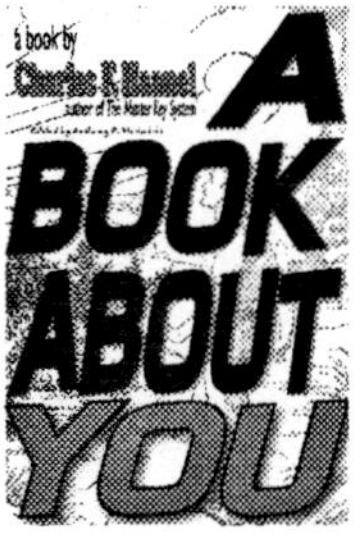

A Book About You
Charles F. Haanel

The New Psychology
Charles F. Haanel

Walk, Don't Run
Steven "Rusty" Johnson

Getting Connected Through Exceptional Leadership
Karl Walinskas

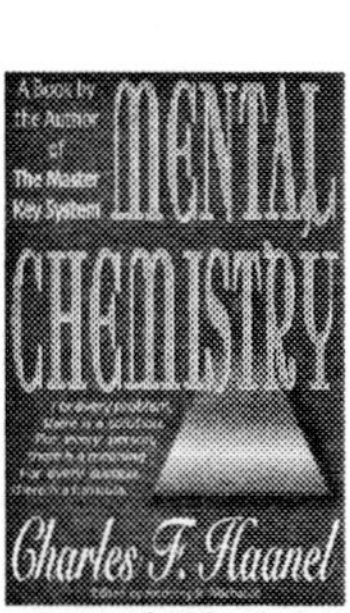

Mental Chemistry
Charles F. Haanel

The Master Key Institute

If you found the ideas and lessons in this book engaging and would like to continue your studies on your path to the attainment of your dreams, then you should learn about **The Master Key Institute**. The information is *free* and you will learn about:

- The Master Key Institute: the authoritative source of Charles F. Haanel's ideas and philosophies and how you can use them to improve your life and attain your dreams.
- The quarterly newsletter, *ATTAIN*, which discusses the lessons with articles by and about very successful people.
- Conference calls that allow you to communicate with seekers like you.
- Phone mentoring with the greatest coaches available anywhere that will work with you to achieve what you desire.
- A special web site that will serve you as a valuable resource for your studies and a place to build your ideas into reality.
- Special offers on seminars, conferences, new releases, CD's, videos, and more.
- An opportunity to earn referral bonuses, with which you really put the Law of Abundance into effect.

This information is yours FREE with no obligation.

Web: **www.themasterkeyinstitute.com**
E-mail: **info@kallistipublishing.com**
Mail: **The Master Key Institute**
332 Center Street
Wilkes-Barre, PA 18702

www.thenewpsychology.com